David Sacks was born in Derbyshire, England. Son of a tailor, he received a grammar school education and later served in the military police in Germany. Subsequently, he became a police constable, later a detective constable, rising to detective chief inspector. He also became a senior special branch officer in Manchester and in 1979 investigated the disappearance of two young Britons in Central America, the subject matter of this book. He lives in Lancashire, is married to Jane and he also has a son and a daughter.

This book is dedicated to the memory of Christopher Farmer and Peta Frampton and also Mary Lou Boston. The dedication is also extended to their bereaved families.

David Sacks

NOTHING MUCH HAPPENS ON A BOAT

AUSTIN MACAULEY PUBLISHERS™

LONDON • CAMBRIDGE • NEW YORK • SHARJAH

A CIP catalogue record for this title is available from the British Library.

ISBN 9781528929790 (Paperback)
ISBN 9781528966009 (ePub e-book)

www.austinmacauley.com

First Published 2021
Austin Macauley Publishers Ltd
Level 37, Office 37.15, 1 Canada Square
Canary Wharf
London
E14 5AA

I must thank the British Foreign and Commonwealth Office without whose huge assistance the fate of Christopher Farmer and Peta Frampton may never have become known. Credit is due to the Greater Manchester Police Cold Case Review Unit's Detective Michaela Clinch and the Unit Head Martin Bottomley. The original murder suspect was finally arrested in the United States of America following great work by Detectives Amy Crosby, Janine LeRose of the Sacramento Police Department, and also FBI Special Agent David Sesma, all assisted by a brilliant team of US Assistant Attorneys, Mathew D Segal, Heiko P Coppola and Jeremy J Kelly, led by US Attorney Philip J Talbert. Accurate reporting of the case by the Sacramento Bee Newspaper and its reporter Peter Hecht is also acknowledged. I owe my dear wife Jane huge gratitude for her help, advice, and also her patience during the many hours involved in the writing of the book. I must apologise in advance for any possible errors although I have endeavoured to tell the story as it was, presenting all the facts available to me as accurately as possible. Credit must be given to Penny Farmer for her decision, in 2015, to ask that this very old cold case be re-opened. Finally, Vince Boston and his brother Russell who were the principal means by which the case was solved. I also owe gratitude to Vince, during our communications, for his consent to use various photographs, and also for the additional information that he supplied.

Chapter One
The Phone Call

I had been retired from the Police for some 28 years when, in the early afternoon of 5th October, 2015, I was relaxing at home when the telephone rang. I picked up the handset and the caller identified herself as Michaela Clinch, a detective with the Cold Case Unit of the Greater Manchester Police (GMP). She asked if I could confirm I had been the detective who had investigated the double murder of two young Britons in Guatemala over 36 years previously. The case Detective Clinch was referring to was one that had, in the first instance, started as a missing person's enquiry but transpired to reveal that the missing couple had been brutally murdered. The victims were a young British man and woman whose bodies were subsequently found in Guatemala. I had investigated the circumstances of the case in which it did appear that the Guatemalan Police had very oddly not become involved after the bodies were discovered. Following my own enquiries and due to the question of jurisdiction and the need for urgent further enquiries in the United States (US), the matter was passed to US Law Enforcement who, it was thought, had jurisdiction. However, following what appeared to have been a somewhat limited investigation there into what was a very grave matter, no arrest followed, the investigation there stalled and the case went cold.

My heart certainly skipped a beat or two when the Manchester detective told me what her call was about. On confirming that I had indeed been the original investigating officer, I wondered, after the passage of so many years, just what was coming. Detective Clinch then told me that Penelope Farmer (Penny) the younger sister of the murdered male victim, Christopher Farmer, had been talking about the case a short time earlier with her elderly widowed mother, Audrey Farmer. As a result of that conversation, Penny was left feeling hugely discontented at the way the case appeared to have been handled and left hanging all those years with no one ever having been brought to book. Penny, a clearly very intelligent and determined woman resolved to do something about it and finally decided to contact the GMP to ask that the case be re-opened.

Detective Clinch explained to me that, as a result of Penny's request, she had visited and spoken with Audrey Farmer who was then aged 91 years. It was most fortunate that Audrey still recalled that the Manchester detective who had originally dealt with the case was called Sacks. Detective Clinch quickly discovered that no one then serving in the GMP had any knowledge whatever about the case due to the passage of so many years. Everyone serving at the time had of course retired. The usual maximum period that a young British Police recruit would then go on to serve, to qualify for a full pension, was about 30 years. My own investigations had commenced 37 years previously, in late 1978. Detective Clinch had presumably traced me via the police pensions department. My son David, also a retired Manchester police inspector could be quickly discounted because he was too young at the time. Detective Clinch was no doubt rather relieved to discover that, as I was drawing my police pension, I was still alive.

She asked me what I might be able to recall about the case and I replied that I could tell her pretty much everything about the main facts as it had been one so very much out of the ordinary. I told her I could recall all the most important and principal details extremely well. I then started to outline the story to her over the phone but then I paused to point out that all the original documents concerning the case were filed at Greater Manchester police headquarters in the Criminal Investigation Administration Department. She then explained to me that the original file could not be located. During the period of some 28 years since I retired, the file had either been *lost* in the archives, perhaps misfiled, or may actually have been routinely, but wrongly *weeded out* and destroyed. Of course the Police, in common with very many organisations, have a policy of weeding out certain old documents and files and destroying them after a certain number of years have passed. That is because few organisations can be expected to keep everything indefinitely, particularly documents that are thought to be of no further use. Files relating to old undetected murders and other very serious crimes are usually routinely retained virtually indefinitely though. Whatever the reason, the original substantial file of documents, containing absolutely everything known about the case, could not be found. The result was that I appeared to be the only person on the planet who might know anything of real value about it.

On being told about the missing file, I, therefore, continued describing aspects of the case to the detective when something suddenly hit me and I stopped talking and said, "Wait a minute, not only can I tell you all about the case, I can do a lot better than that. I've still got my old working copy of the original file here somewhere." There was silence on the line for a few seconds and Detective Clinch said, "Pardon?" I then went on to explain to her how I had, from the start of my involvement, photocopied all the main case documents that came into my possession or that I instigated myself. That was in order to create a *working copy* so as not to have to continuously handle the original documents. Some of them, I perceived, might just be required as court exhibits if a crime was found to have been the cause of the young couple's disappearance. The possibility that they might have been murdered was what I had in mind.

Detective Clinch, obviously clearly rather taken aback at hearing that totally unexpected news, said, "And you still have your copy file after all these years?" she continued, "What exactly is in the documents you have?" I answered, "Everything, a copy of absolutely everything that was on the original headquarters file." I went on to tell her that the copied documents were somewhere at my home although I had not actually seen them for many years following our last house move. She said, "So can I see it?" I responded by saying she could of course, have it. An arrangement was then made for her to drive over to my home to collect the thick file of these old copied documents that had suddenly become something of prospective importance. That is, I thought, she could have the documents when I discovered just where they actually were.

As soon as I put down the phone I, at once, went to the place where I was confident the file would be but was quickly dismayed to find it was not there. I then looked elsewhere, indeed I looked all over in the house, including the loft, with the same result. Beginning to despair considerably after my conversation with Detective Clinch, and wondering if the file had somehow been thrown out, I suddenly had an idea. I went outside to my garden shed at the rear of the house. I unlocked the door and went inside to specifically look inside two cardboard boxes that I knew had actually lain there in a corner undisturbed since my wife and I had moved into the house some 17 years earlier. The boxes were both full of what was more or less junk, most, or all of which really ought to have been discarded years earlier. My despair continued as, not finding it in the first box, I worked my way down through the second one. Then, there it was, right at the very bottom, of course! Deeply thankful, I grabbed it and took it into the house. It all felt rather damp, somewhat smelly and a lot of the pages within the deteriorating outer folder, particularly those towards the bottom, were discoloured and, being damp, were beginning to stick together. However, I carefully peeled the pages apart and laid them all out in the conservatory where they quickly started to curl up as they dried, it being a fairly warm sunny day. I was delighted, and very much relieved to find that everything on all the documents was still entirely legible. I realised though, that once I had handed over those documents, I would most probably never see them again. I, therefore, went up to my study and spent some considerable time, and a lot of paper re-copying everything all over again. Also, being an amateur photographer, I decided to photograph every sheet so that the whole copy file of documents was additionally secured on my digital camera's SD card.

The next day I handed over the complete file of papers to Detective Clinch when she drove to my home. We then sat and talked a good deal more about the case details. I could not help but notice that, as we talked, she, from time to time, kept looking down and lifting up various pages and glancing down at them as though half disbelieving what she had suddenly got possession of. Then off she went back to her office in Manchester, probably somewhat stunned but elated and still finding it a little hard to believe what had transpired. Having been asked to re-open a very old murder case, and not being able to find the original case papers, and thus seemingly facing an impossible task, and then to suddenly be presented with a complete copy of everything thought to have been lost, was, of course, a totally unexpected turn of events. In truth, it was probably a completely unique event! However, I was more than just a little aware that re-opening a cold case is one thing, but getting a successful result that was not originally obtainable, is quite another. Also, I well knew that the British Police could still not actually prosecute anyone themselves, as had been the case so many years before. If anything positive was concluded by the Cold Case Unit, it would still be a matter for US Law Enforcement to follow up, that is of course if they could be persuaded to do so. That old deteriorating file of copied papers I handed over to Detective Clinch, that in reality should never have still existed at all, was in the event, going to prove to be rather important, which I must confess is a rather large and very deliberate understatement.

The fact that those copy documents still existed following their creation some 36 years earlier was one thing. That they ever actually finished up and remained at my home, and finally, rather to my continuing huge embarrassment, actually in my garden shed, was another. That I ever got to have possession of them at all was because, on my last day of police service on 14th April 1987, I was in the process of clearing my desk and office. I came across the copy file at the bottom of a cabinet drawer. I didn't then even know how come I had it as I had never ever made any conscious decision to retain it. The folder containing the file had actually mixed in amongst some other papers in my office. As I was preparing to leave the Police Station for the last time, my wastepaper basket was already stuffed full and overflowing so it certainly wouldn't fit in or on there so I initially just put it down on my desk wondering what to do with it. I was not inclined to start shredding the very thick pile of papers before I departed so I finished up putting the file in a cardboard box along with my personal items, deciding that I would burn it or shred it at my home later. However, the destruction of these seemingly useless documents never happened and I cannot explain why not. I much later somehow could not bring myself to do so. I recall at one time, picking up the file, looking at some of the pages and thinking about destroying it but it passed through my mind that what I was looking at were all the known facts about the brutal murder of two young people. It somehow just seemed far too important to destroy so I closed the pages and put the file back in the cardboard box. During the next few years and until I retired, the file very oddly just seemed to follow me! And the documents eventually somehow finished up laying, and deteriorating, at the bottom of a damp cardboard box in my garden shed. It was as though, without me thinking about it, those documents were just waiting for the time when they were very unexpectedly, and rather

15

urgently going to be needed again. I have the extremely odd feeling that the reason I actually took the file home but never got around to destroying it, and then retained it for so many years, was because somehow, fate had determined that those documents were never actually 'meant' to be destroyed! And those papers were indeed going to be needed again very many years after the murders. Perhaps this may all seem just a bit silly coming from a rather hardbitten old police officer but I still have the distinctly odd feeling that all things considered, the continuing existence of that file of papers was all just a little bit spooky!

Chapter Two
A Trip to Tragedy

Christopher Farmer was a medical doctor and Peta Frampton a lawyer. They had both studied and, at the time, had fairly recently graduated from Birmingham University in England. An easygoing, happy and attractive couple, Christopher was 25 years of age and Peta 24. They had known one another since childhood, having lived on the same road. They were obviously very close and enjoyed one another's company a great deal. Their respective parents were friends too. Christopher and Peta were British citizens and their family homes were in the north of England. As young energetic adults, with their enormously valuable academic achievements recently secured, and with very promising futures, they faced it with their whole lives ahead of them, and with all that it might bring, success, marriage, children.

Soon after their hard-won graduations, they decided, in the latter part of 1977, to embark on a touring holiday before settling down seriously to their new professions. Part of the holiday was intended to be a working one. Their vacation started with a journey to Australia, that starting in December 1977, where Christopher then worked for some three months at an after-hours medical service in Brisbane. They in due course intended to return to England after a further period spent visiting various other places. Their holiday was actually destined to end in Central America. Regular communication with their families was of extreme importance to both of them and so there were very frequent letters to their families along with occasional audio tapes and some telephone calls. Peta's letters were usually quite lengthy with diary-like and dated entries that were always full of information such as where they were, had been, what they were doing at the time of writing, and also of their future intentions.

Towards the intended end of their holiday, a letter was received from Peta by her parents in England to the effect that they were in Belize, Central America. The last dated entry in that letter was 13th June 1978 shortly after they had arrived there. Her letter described how they had just met a man called *Dwayne* who was the owner and skipper of a sailing boat, *The Justin B*, that he had purchased just a few weeks earlier. *Dwayne* was an American citizen whose full name was later revealed to be Silas Duane Boston, then aged 37 years. He was at the time accompanied on his boat by his two sons Vince then aged 13, and Russell, a year or two younger. *The Justin B*, originally a wooden six-ton fishing vessel had been converted to a pleasure sailing boat shortly before Boston acquired it. The vessel, it was later learned, had been jointly paid for by Boston and his father Russell Boston senior, who lived in California in the US. That said, his father had never seen the boat.

Reproduced below is an extract from Peta's last but one letter containing the first mention of Boston and his boat, *The Justin B*:

FIRST MENTION OF BOSTON AND THE JUSTIN B

to (Merida) but knew an American called
Dwayne who owns a belizian boat called
the "Justin B" offered to take us up to
Chetumal by sail so we decided to do
that. I'm now in Sarteneja on the north
coast of Belize & tomorrow we go on to

Peta and Christopher, in conversation with Boston shortly after meeting him, having changed their original travel plans, told him of their desire to travel to Puerto Cortes in Honduras. Boston then offered to take them there on *The Justin B*. From Puerto Cortes they were going to leave the area. Peta then intended to travel on to the US where she wanted to meet up with a friend before going back to England. She wrote of hoping to find some temporary casual work whilst in the US to earn some money. Christopher seemingly intended to return directly to England, presumably to commence work there in his profession. Boston, in agreeing to carry them to Puerto Cortes would obviously have charged them for the trip and it is assumed that a fee would have been discussed. An arrangement having been made, the five of them first sailed south down the coast of Belize to a place Peta referred to as Placentia (actually Placencia). From there the intention was to sail in a generally easterly direction to Puerto Cortes. Peta and Christopher shared a tiny two bunk cabin on *The Justin B*, that cabin also served as the boat's galley. Boston and his sons shared the other larger cabin.

Another eight-page handwritten letter from Peta, with the envelope, postmarked 18th July 1978, at Livingston, Guatemala, was received by her family in August of that year. The photocopied postmark on the envelope containing the letter is reproduced below, followed by a printed copy of exactly what she wrote in that letter. I photographed the original letter's envelope with its postmark and then enlarged the area of the envelope showing the postmarked date itself. That was because the postmark proved to be unreadable when I tried to simply photocopy it. I then printed and photocopied the very much clearer photograph:

THE POSTMARK

"On the way to Hunting Cay
28.6.78.

Dear Mum

We have just set off from Placentia, a small fishing port in the south of Belize and it's abt 7 am. The sun is warm, the sky is a little cloudy and the sea is emerald green and somewhat choppy so my writing may go haywire. Placentia is very pretty. It can only be reached by four-wheel drive and is built on sand with a narrow cement pathway linking the houses etc. When we arrived from Stann Creek we were longing for ice-cold beer as usual (sailing makes you thirsty and we didn't have much water onboard) but there was no beer or soft drinks in town. The Belizeans don't grow vegetables which are grown by the Meunoiures in the west of the country. Cauliflower can cost $5 so we have been living on corned beef and baked beans, and of course rice and beans and fish when we can catch them. We had to spend nearly a week at Stann Creek trying to get extra ballast. Finally, we were given abt 700 lbs by a white Belizean who is the general manager of the Belizean Citrus Co at Pomona abt 12 miles from Stann Creek. He gave us a tour of the factory V, impressive. They make concentrated orange juice and tinned grapefruit most of which goes to the UK under the name of "Trout hall". Have you seen any? He gave us a few tins - v. gd for breakfast tho', you know, I don't like it much. We had to get a whole load of papers stamped for customs clearance and paid $10 which went straight into the officer's pocket, of course. In Belize City, we had to pay $86 BH for entry papers into Honduras. It seems that there is nothing but hassle and money to go anywhere by boat. Chris has been doing a lot of sailing and even I have taken the tiller a few times - v. tiring depending on the strength of the wind.

29.6.78. Well, we had a perfect sail, Chris wants me to say that this was due to his superb navigation (with only a $5 compass) and reached Hunting Cay abt 11 am. This Cay is v. pretty. The only person who lives on it (it's only 500 yds x 100 yds) is the lighthouse keeper. We were surprised to see the pelicans (everywhere here—but not pretty as they're

21

brown) roosting in the coconut palms. With the wonders of modern civilisation, this would be an idyllic Caribbean island. We've docked only about 50 yds offshore and the water is perfectly clear. There's reef some way off, and another 4 Cays visible. We caught a lobster and sardines last night. I was v. pleased yesterday when I managed to make some "fry-jack" a flatbread fried in the pan. I'd only watched Tom, the sailor I told you about, to make it once, and he was a baker. Talking to the lighthouse keeper, this is the worst time for sailing and our next sail to Porto Cortes in Honduras would be very hard so it seems. We may easily decide to go to Livingston in Guatemala instead which is a simple sail with the wind behind us. If we do, I shall leave *The Justin B* and get a ferry to Porto Cortes and a plane from Honduras to New Orleans. I am getting a bit weary of the practical difficulties of living on this tiny boat with four other people. At least I managed to get a shower in Placentia by throwing buckets of well water over me. I think I'm getting too old for primitive living. Like all boats, this one has cockroaches. We sleep in the galley, a space of abt 4' x 5' x 2½' and it's horrible when we turn out the kerosene lamp and they come out. We spray Baygon every day but they come out to die! I don't mind cockroaches that much, there were loads in Morocco and Australia but I like a little space between me and them. Another reason I wouldn't mind ending my sailing career now—I'm down as a sailor on the papers—is the two sons of Duane. They are 12 and 13 years but behave more like 8 or 9 and I find I have no patience at all with them. Of course, they squabble most of the time and I now see how irritating it must have been in that respect. But on a boat there's nowhere you can go. What makes it worse is that Duane curses and puts them down continuously, often when things are not going quite right, like when we didn't get one of the anchors up because the motor wasn't working to give us leverage and we subsequently went back for it and managed to retrieve it, abt £100 worth.

Did I tell you I managed to get two little pieces of black coral in Sarteneja! tiny but wld look nice suspended by a gold link on a chain. I was shown some beautiful tortoiseshell bracelets, v. common and inexpensive here and illegal to import into the US, but I didn't get anything, as usual, they were all too big for me.

Time seems to go very quickly here—it's nearly July already. It must be getting quite warm in England. I hope you've been swimming. Did I hear that there's going to be a general election? I haven't seen a newspaper for weeks and the BBC World News doesn't give much abt the UK. I often wonder what everyone is doing and I feel v. cut off but letters are too difficult as I never know where I'm going to be next. I'm already a month late at Tause in N.O. but I'm looking forward to getting there as the music's supposed to be excellent in the pubs there. Of course, it'll be abt 30 degrees and v. humid but I guess I've gotten a bit used to it all and it makes a lot of difference having a shower etc. I don't know how long I'll be able to stay there, it all depends how money lasts but afterwards, I want to visit an English friend who's just started a two-year contract in Columbia Maryland, not far from Washington DC. I've also been vaguely offered a job by a diver (female) in San Diego Calif, so I may go down there later if it seems I can earn some money. On my US visa it says, I'm not permitted to work but it seems that it's not too difficult getting casual jobs and that's what I hope to do if possible. Enough of the future. I don't think there's any more news—nothing much happens on a boat."

Lots of love Pete.

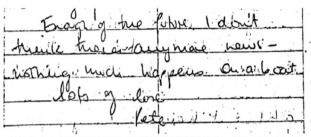

THE LAST WORDS OF PETA'S LAST LETTER

The idyllic tiny island of Hunting Cay is a place most people might think of as a typical desert island. In modern times it has become quite a popular place to visit for tourists in the area. *The Justin B* stopped at the island and remained there for an overnight stop on 28th June 1978. Puerto Cortes was still some distance away and obviously could not be reached before dark. The island lies to the south of a long chain of such islands, or Cays, known as the Spodella Islands. Hunting Cay is mostly covered with palm trees and the surrounding waters teem with an enormous variety of sea life. The island is roughly 400 metres or so long and, at its narrowest, a mere 100 metres. Boats visiting there usually drop anchor in a small bay on the eastern side of the island. The old lighthouse there, referred to by Peta in her letter, was later replaced by an automatic light on a tower. Various photographs of the island can be viewed on the web.

After the receipt of Peta's letter by her family in August 1978, with its 18th July postmarked envelope, nothing further was heard from the pair. As one week then ran to another with no further communication, the Farmer and Frampton families, very understandably, began to worry considerably. That developed into a much deeper concern that something might be seriously wrong as the lack of any contact continued. There had actually occurred a previous break in communication that caused similar concern but then a letter was received, the last but one, resulting in relief from the two families' worries. There then followed the second break in communication causing renewed worries to the families but when Peta's last letter, dated 18th June 1978 was gratefully received the following August, that worry had similarly ended, leastwise temporarily.

There is no room for doubt, as a result of the information in Peta's final letter, that *The Justin B* had indeed stopped off at Hunting Cay whilst en route to their intended destination of Puerto Cortes. They would have reached the island just a few hours after setting off from Placencia on the morning of 28th June. They were still moored just a few yards off the island at 11 am on 29th. Peta wrote of having managed to catch a lobster and some sardines the previous evening.

Peta's letter additionally communicated that whilst at Hunting Cay they had met and spoken with the island's only resident, that being the lighthouse keeper. On telling him of their plan to sail from there to Puerto Cortes in Honduras, some 30 or so miles away, he had advised against it, referring to it as a *difficult* sail. Doubtless, he meant by that adverse weather, sea, or wind, or a combination of existing or expected sailing conditions at that particular time. As a result, Peta wrote that they might therefore easily change their minds about sailing on to Puerto Cortes and instead do an easy sail to Livingston, with the wind behind them. From Livingston, the intention was then to catch a (commercial) ferry to Puerto Cortes. It seems most probable that they would have sailed from Hunting Cay sometime during the late morning or early afternoon of 29th June.

My copy of Peta's letter, with its postmark and the information it contained, was later to prove of critical importance in enabling the tracking of the pair's most relevant movements. It thus greatly assisted my original enquiries and was eventually to lead on to the discovery of what had happened to them. Peta's original letter and its envelope had of course been on the Police file that had been lost.

Following the absence of any further communication following receipt of that last letter in August, Christopher's father, Charles Farmer, and also Audrey started to make their own enquiries in an effort to try to trace the pair. Mr Farmer had a long journalistic background, including having worked for the British Broadcasting Corporation (BBC). Charles was a well-educated, highly intelligent and articulate individual. During his own determined, desperate and quite exhaustive enquiries, he had regular contact with the British Foreign and Commonwealth Office (FCO) both by telephone and letters, requesting enquiries in the area where they were last known to have been. The two families' initial concern was that the couple might have been the victims of some crime, or maybe had been involved in an accident, fallen foul of the local law and possibly thrown in jail somewhere with no means of communicating. Even kidnapping was considered a possibility, a problem by no means unknown in that part of the world. Guatemala had a very serious crime problem in those days. Indeed, the country remains crimeridden and it is reported that in 2012, on average, there were almost one hundred murders every week nationwide. Armed robbery, gang culture and extortion are widespread with the authorities unable to control or even alleviate the situation.

Charles Farmer at one point hired a private detective to make enquiries in the area and he also wrote to the editor of a local newspaper there but all his efforts at that time were to no avail. What had caused all communications from Christopher and Peta to abruptly cease, remained a complete mystery. All that was known with certainty was they were last known to be on Boston's Justin B at Hunting Cay on the morning of Thursday 29th June 1978, having an almost certain intention to head for Livingston. Charles Farmer was finally advised by the FCO that the two families should go to the Police. Obviously, that was because they feared that some serious harm had indeed befallen the couple.

Chapter Three
Initial Enquiries

On Monday 30th October 1978, Mrs Audrey Farmer along with Mr John Frampton, Peta's father, went to the GMP's Divisional Headquarters at Stretford and reported the circumstances to Detective Sergeant Michael Carter whom I knew. He and his superior officers at Stretford saw that there were obvious international considerations involved, and so it was decided to refer the case to GMP's Headquarters for a decision as to exactly how investigations might be taken forward. It was suggested that Special Branch might take on the case.

I had been a police officer since 1957, following my service with the British Army where I had served in the Military Police in Germany. I became a detective after five years as a uniformed constable with the Lancashire Constabulary and in 1968, I was promoted detective sergeant shortly after my involvement in a successful murder investigation. I became detective inspector in 1974 when parts of Lancashire were incorporated with Manchester, to become the GMP. I was promoted to detective chief inspector in 1976. In the latter three ranks, I was a supervisor of various teams of detectives in different, very busy areas. I thus gained considerable experience, having been involved in many serious criminal offences, including murders, sexual and other assaults, child kidnapping, blackmail, burglaries, etc. I was, in due course, invited to serve in Special Branch. I accepted the offer and was seconded to Special Branch and then based at the GMP's Headquarters in 1978.

It might be wondered just why a missing persons' case, even one such as this, was actually referred to my particular department at police headquarters. It might very reasonably be thought that any divisional detective could have been expected to carry out the necessary and obvious enquiries that I was tasked with, and did. I would certainly agree with such a view but, as things transpired, had the case not been passed to me, what needed to happen many years later, would undoubtedly have been very much different, or, more likely, quite impossible. What I mean by this is that not only did I decide to copy all the original documents, which not everyone does, but I also, almost accidentally, kept possession of those copies, then retained them for very many years. That is something that, I'm virtually certain, would never have occurred had any other detective originally dealt with the case.

Special Branch is a part of the police service that only very rarely would become involved in any enquiries relating to missing persons. That is unless there was some perceived connection with what might be termed its 'normal' work. Much of the routine work of Special Branch concentrates on matters involving National Security, including Terrorism and what might be termed 'political extremism'. The department regularly liaises closely with the nation's Security Services in that regard. The branch also has other routine areas of work, including dealing with matters concerning foreign nationals, and also conducting armed close protection of people such as members of the British royal family, government ministers and foreign government dignitaries when they visit various events and locations such as Manchester, where I worked. A good deal of Special Branch work is classified as secret and all its staff are subject to the most intense security vetting.

Despite it being deemed a missing persons' enquiry, because of the obvious concerns, my department chief agreed that we would look into the matter and I was the officer tasked to deal with it. It would not be truthful of me if I were to say I was at the time particularly happy to be given a task that I felt could really have been dealt with other than by the department I was working in. Be that as it may, the job was mine and my first move was to arrange to quickly meet up with Charles Farmer. I could not help but be extremely impressed with him from the outset. He was a remarkable and likeable man and was a true gentleman. We initially spoke at considerable length about all the known circumstances and our relationship was to develop into a very easy and very friendly one. Because of Mr Farmer's personality and journalistic background, I discovered, from an early stage, that I was able to confide in him far more than I would have normally in such circumstances.

His objectivity was extraordinary despite his deep personal anxiety. He brought to our first meeting all the documents and correspondence in his possession up to that time, both outgoing and incoming and he handed all these over to me. The papers included Peta's last two letters, the latter one proved to be the most important document by far. What I could not avoid thinking from the outset was that the disappearance of the young couple was very likely the consequence of some serious criminal offence. After Mr Farmer left, I set about photocopying all the documents he had handed over to me, the originals being then filed away in the headquarters' administration department. The reason I did this was that I knew that if it proved to be the case that the missing pair were indeed the victims of a serious crime, and I thought that is what had probably happened, then some of the original documents would be needed as exhibits in any ensuing Criminal Court case. Therefore, to continually have to handle them whilst working on the case, was not a good idea. The photocopies I made became my 'working copy', obviating the alternative need to handle the originals. In the event, they were somehow destined to be lost anyway. I was also given sight of, and read, Charles Farmer's own handwritten and comprehensive 'log' of everything he had learned, that included his actions and thoughts during his own enquiries up to that point in time. His log, in the main, contained information that was contained within the documents he had handed to me. After photocopying his log, I handed the original back to him as he wished to retain it, presumably so he could update it with any further developments. I did not finally see a need to keep the photocopied log with my working copy after I had obtained a written witness statement from Charles Farmer so it went in the original (lost) Headquarters' file. Anything that Charles had written in his log that I considered of possible evidential value was included within his witness statement. As I created and received further documents, those were also photocopied. The original file and my own working copy of it thus became quite substantial in thickness.

After my initial meeting with Charles Farmer and reviewing all the known facts from the documents, I commenced enquiries by making contact with Interpol and also the British FCO in London. Indeed, all my written enquiries to the FCO were normally required, by protocol, to be done via Interpol, other than some telephone calls that I decided I really needed to make directly to avoid delays. Written and spoken material routinely passing via Interpol often did lead to frustrating delays and additionally to some occasional annoying misunderstandings as to exactly what I wanted to get done by people several thousands of miles away. The matter of who did or did not have legal jurisdiction in the case seemed not to be fully understood by everyone I communicated with.

In my personal contacts with the FCO by letter and, in the latter stages, particularly by telephone, I requested renewed determined specific enquiries to trace the couple, and of course, the particularly urgent need to trace the whereabouts of the American, Silas Duane Boston. He seemed to have disappeared and I could only wonder whether Boston had actually fled the area rather than just having moved on. It transpired that he had indeed left the area and a Belize Port, the official report showed that *The Justin B* had sailed into Dangriga on 9th August 1978. A report by the Harbourmaster at the Belize Port Authority Office was revealed sometime later, dated 31st December 1978 stating that *The Justin B* was then sold at Sarteneja on 14 August some 120 miles north of Dangriga, that being roughly when Peta's last letter was received by her family. The Harbourmaster also stated that *The Justin B* had then been renamed, presumably by its new owners. Boston had actually owned *The Justin B* for a relatively short period of time. I had wondered if the sale of the boat might have been somewhat hurried and connected with the disappearance of Christopher and Peta but then saw that she had written that Boston had mentioned selling the boat.

Fortunately, the information contained in Peta's last letter made it pretty clear where enquiries could realistically be concentrated. It came to light, during the further enquiries I requested of the FCO, that a Father Gerry of the Claretian Fathers based in Santo Tomas in Guatemala, had heard of a rumour that clearly needed following up as a matter of urgency. The story he heard of was that some local fishermen had apparently been talking about the unidentified bodies of a man and a woman having been found floating in the sea some 200 metres offshore at some remote location. The place spoken of was revealed to be Punta de Manabique that I saw lay on a peninsular across Amatique Bay some ten miles north from Livingston. The map of the area also showed me that Punta de Manabique lay on a virtually straight line between Hunting Cay and Livingston. The date of the reported finding of the bodies was at first wrongly stated as sometime in September 1978 and that initially served to confuse matters somewhat. When what Father Gerry had learned was picked up by the FCO and then relayed to me, I at once requested further urgent enquiries by them to establish firstly, if the information was reliable, and secondly, if so, what happened to the reported found bodies. The further enquiries I requested, revealed shortly afterwards that the information was indeed confirmed and that date of the finding of the bodies was actually Saturday 8th July 1978, not in September of that year, as I had earlier been led to believe.

Punta de Manabique was a very small and remote settlement or village situated on the southern tip of a peninsular that was called Tres Puntas. Livingston, and Punta de Manabique and Amatique Bay were all within Guatemalan territory. The peninsular is a jungle and mangrove swamp-covered and is very sparsely populated. Along most of the coastline of the peninsular, the jungle grows almost right down to the edge of the sea. Thus, anyone wanting to go ashore along most of the length of the shoreline there was then faced with that thick jungle and swamps with not much in the way of civilisation in the interior, other than Punta de Manabique itself and a few scattered dwellings.

I learned that when found, the bodies were in an advanced state of decomposition. That indicated to me that they had obviously been in the water for at least a number of days. I guessed probably of the order of a week. It was very clear that those two unidentified people had been murdered. Both were found with their arms and hands firmly bound behind their backs and the legs and ankles of each of them were similarly secured. Further, both completely immobilised bodies were attached by lengths of ropes to pieces of what were described as heavy metal machinery or automotive parts. The female, for some then-unknown reason, was found to have a plastic bag tied over her head. Initial reports by those involved in recovering the bodies suggested that the man might have been shot in the right leg, and perhaps also in the chest and that both bodies seemed to show signs of what was vaguely described as other 'injuries'. There was also a suggestion that some of the perceived injuries were suggestive of torture. There was nothing to identify who they were. After a Post Mortem examination, carried out two days after the bodies were found, both were then buried, still unidentified, in adjacent numbered graves in the cemetery of a town called Puerto Barrios. Reproduced below is a copy of the official translated report that I received, prepared by one of the parties of men (Bomberos) involved in the recovery of the bodies:

CUERPO VOLUNTARIO DE BOMBEROS DE GUATEMALA
REPORT OF MISCELLANEOUS SERVICES

Control Nº   Minutes worked: 385
Telephone request Nº BANDEGUA Personal: Date: 8 July 1978
Departure from: 7th Company Hour: 11.35 Entrance at: 7th Company
Hour: 18.15
Address: Punta de Manabique
Name of applicant: Justice of the Peace of this port.
Type of service: Transfer of corpse
Unit Nº 78 Driver: Bombero Juan René Sorto
Radio/telephone operator: Bombero 2nd Félix Dardón Torres
Detached personnel: Bombero 3rd Marco Tulio Loyo Ortega, Bombero
    3rd Rudy Alicio Palacios

REMARKS:

At the request of the Justice of the Peace of this port, we were
transported by a unit of the Marines to Punta de Manabique. On
arrival at the place mentioned we became aware that approximately
200 meters from the beach two corpses were floating in the sea. We
had to go into the water, since we had already attempted to lift them
from the deck of a small boat supplied by local commissioners. When
we were in the water we became aware that one of them, the male, was
wearing a blue canvas jacket and blue shorts, the body was decomposed
and we could not obtain major details of complexion, hair, face, etc.
This corpse had its hands bound behind the back and legs and ankles
were also bound; round the neck it had a yellow nylon string 15 meters
long tied to a "shock-block" (part of the engine of an automobile),
it had a bullet hole in the right leg and signs of torture. The other
corpse, the female, was wearing a green T-shirt, no brassiere, green
shorts, and was also decomposed; her hands were bound in the back
as were her legs and ankles, and from the string in the bottom of the
sea hung part of the engine of an automobile commonly called "Espejo
con toda y su corona". She had a plastic bag covering her head, as
a hood, tied around her neck, and it was observed that her hair was
blonde, her age was between 15 and 18 years, 1.65 meters high.
After picking up the bodies they were taken from Punta de Manabique
to the dock of the Marines at Santo Tomás and from there to the
Puerto Barrios National Amphitheatre in Unit 78 of this Company.

Report made by: Bombero Marco Tulio Loyo
Seen by driver: Bombero Juan René Sorto
Approved. Official in Service: Of. Gustavo Guerra

BOMBEROS' RECOVERY OF THE BODIES REPORT

It was obvious that if the found bodies were those of Christopher Farmer and Peta Frampton, and I strongly suspected that they were, establishing whether that was true or not could only be achieved by me after first seeking the exhumation the bodies. Whether the Guatemalan authorities would actually be prepared to authorise the necessary exhumations was entirely another matter. I was at the time led to believe that after the burial there, a body could not be *moved* until a period of four years had elapsed. Whether that also applied to exhumations, I did not know. If it did, it looked as though we would have to wait for some three more years for exhumations.

With all that in mind, I anyway enquired as to where Christopher and Peta might have received dental treatment and it transpired that they both had dental work carried out at Birmingham University during the time they had been studying there. The University Dental Department supplied me with the respective dental charts and I sent them on to Guatemala via Interpol and the FCO. I included, with the charts, a detailed report urgently requesting that, as the case was clearly one of murder, the Guatemalan authorities authorise the exhumations. I asked that an examination and comparison be made, by a dental expert there, between the forwarded dental charts and the teeth of the two bodies I wanted to be exhumed. That process being desired, there was considerable concern that should the Guatemala authorities simply refuse my request for exhumations, I would likely be faced with a serious problem. If the buried bodies were to remain unidentified where they lay, proving what had happened to Christopher and Peta would have likely been quite impossible, that is unless somehow other avenues became available. That said, whoever the recovered bodies were, an absolutely dreadful crime had been committed.

Soon afterwards though, I was informed in a letter from the FCO that my requested exhumations had been authorised and had taken place on Tuesday 10th April 1979, that being some nine months after the bodies were found. A positive identification had been made, during what must have been a most unpleasant task, by a Guatemalan Dental Surgeon, Doctor Gustavo Berger Reyes who had stated that it was his firm opinion that the previously unidentified bodies were indeed those of Christopher and Peta. Doctor Reyes afterwards compiled a report to that effect. He had made his own dental charts during the examination of each of the bodies at the gravesites and then carried out careful comparisons of his own charts with those I had sent.

The Doctor's comprehensive report, dated Monday 16th April 1979, was then forwarded to me. To finally confirm things, I took Doctor Reyes' report, along with its translation, and the British and Guatemala dental charts, and handed them to Doctor James Holt, a consultant dental surgeon, at Manchester University Dental Hospital. Doctor Holt, in his own report dated Friday 8th June 1979, confirmed Doctor Reyes' findings absolutely. The families were actually given the extremely distressing news in a letter from the FCO as soon as they saw Doctor Reyes' report. Doctor Reyes made a little sketch of the area within the cemetery where the bodies were interred. A copy of what is actually a simple but truly poignant sketch is reproduced below, the respective graves Doctor Reyes marked 'he' and 'she', are indicated.

As the bodies had been found and recovered from the sea early in the morning of Saturday, 8th July 1978, some other person had, of course, posted Peta's letter postmarked 18th July in Livingston. From the decomposing condition of the bodies, it was fairly obvious that they had been murdered on or quite soon after Thursday the 29th June 1978, the last dated entry in Peta's letter. The question was just who posted the letter? The last known positive location of that letter, prior to posting, was either aboard *The Justin B* or possibly ashore at Hunting Cay was on the 29th June. It was reasonable to presume that it was posted by the murderer to give the completely false impression to the families back in England that the pair were alive on 18th July, sometime after Boston would later claim to have parted company with them. The families of course, on receiving the letter, were induced to initially believe exactly that. My own view was that Boston, after killing them, had discovered, kept and then deliberately posted the letter over two weeks after he killed them, for that very purpose.

Peta and Christopher were very much alive during at least part of the 29th June, and so, considering the decomposing state of the bodies when recovered on Saturday 8th July, I concluded that they must have been murdered either later on 29th or on the 30th of June 1978, but if not then, very shortly after those two days. It was reported that the bodies were discovered floating just below the surface and had been spotted, quite by chance, by Mr Ezequiel Ramirez who happened to be the Deputy Mayor of the tiny village of Punta de Manabique and who had fortunately been passing that exact spot in another small boat. The Bomberos team who were called out to recover the bodies found that some fifteen-metre lengths of rope were securing the bodies to each of the weights. Whilst the weights were sufficient to hold the victims firmly below the surface, the ropes were obviously not sufficiently short so as to have kept the bodies more deeply under the surface. In that event, the bodies might otherwise have been completely hidden from view. Fortunately, the bodies were visible to Mr Ramirez who just happened to look down into the water whilst passing the spot. It was possible to discount the fact that the bodies came into view because the tide had dropped, as I was told that the tides in that area are minimal and rarely rise and fall much more than a foot or two, and most frequently rather less than that. It may also be the case that extremely clear water may have also contributed to the bodies being visible not far below the surface. It was, at one point, thought that the bodies, as they decomposed, might have become increasingly buoyant due to the internal production of gasses and in the process had perhaps lifted the weights off the sea bottom and thus had floated towards the surface. That was discounted because, had that been the case, the bodies would no doubt have drifted apart whereas they were still close together in the water. Whatever the reason for them being visible to the passing Deputy Mayor, they had been found despite the obvious intention of their murderer. It was erroneously suggested and reported at some later stage that the bodies had been found after washing ashore which had not happened.

As a result of what the shocked Mr Ramirez had discovered, the small party of Guatemalan volunteers, called Bomberos, had been called to the location by the local Justice of the Peace. He asserted he made some initial enquiries in the area after the bodies were found. Following what was obviously an extremely horrible and difficult operation, the Bomberos team did recover the bodies that were then taken ashore to Puerto Barrios. Oddly, there was no documentary evidence whatever to indicate that the Guatemalan Police had played any active part at all or indeed if they were actually informed of the finding of the bodies by the Justice of the Peace, or anyone else. It seemed very peculiar for that not to have happened but there was no evidence of it. No one apparently thought to recover the ropes and weights, which might have been unfortunate. Recovery of those items would have been routine if a competent police officer had been involved. I originally thought that, had the ropes and weights been recovered, the possibility might have existed of linking those items to the boat from which they had been put into the sea. Any such possible evidence was lost though, but in the end, it was to be of no consequence. Those substantial heavy metal weights are probably, even now, still lying on the sea bed.

On Monday 10th July 1979, two days after their recovery from the sea, both bodies were made the subject of a post mortem examination and the Doctor/Pathologist involved concluded they had both died of asphyxia by drowning. So, it seemed clear that Christopher and Peta, horrifically, were both alive, and quite probably conscious, when deliberately put into the sea, securely bound, and rendered totally immobile and helpless. The substantial heavyweights, to which they were attached, ensured they remained under the surface as they drowned. Their torment, shock and rapid realisation of their hopeless situation when they went into the water and during their remaining consciousness, and hopeless struggles, is hard to dwell upon. It is an unquestionable fact that drowning happens to be an extremely unpleasant and distressing way to die albeit with complete submersion, mercifully, it does not take very long at all.

Many people believe that drowning is a process whereby someone submerged, after automatically holding their breath as long as they can, are after a short time automatically compelled to try to inhale and thus start to inhale and exhale water instead of air until they die. That is not actually accurate. In complete submersion, after a short period of automatic breathholding, the victim will irresistibly have to try to inhale but the moment that water enters the upper airway, it automatically reacts by closing. Thus, the conscious victim can neither inhale nor exhale although there probably might initially occur a brief coughing or choking effect as the airway attempts to clear itself of water. Some water, though, can actually be drawn into the stomach I understand. Few of us have failed to experience the extremely unpleasant instant reaction we get if, when drinking something, some of the liquid *goes down the wrong way* and gets into our airway. We experience that violent coughing choking effect for a few moments before our airway starts to fully re-open. As it does so, we can still hardly breathe freely, or even speak for a short time, and we will cough and splutter until things return to normal. In drowning, things cannot of course return to normal and the victim quickly starts to asphyxiate. Unconsciousness will usually occur within around three minutes or so due to oxygen starvation to the brain. Death inevitably follows very shortly afterwards as the brain itself dies if submersion continues. There are actually two types of drowning and the one described is known as 'dry drowning' because very little or no water actually enters the lungs. The term 'wet drowning' is when, in a usually unconscious submerged person, the airway opens or remains open sufficiently for some water to be drawn into the lungs.

It will, therefore, be clear that drowning someone deliberately and very systematically, as was clearly the case here, was incredibly wicked and heartless in the extreme. It starkly illustrates the nature of the person who had killed them, someone possessing no apparent conscience or pity whatever. It was as clear a calculated and undeniably premeditated abhorrent act of murder of two innocent young people as it is possible to imagine. Whoever did it could properly be described as a monster or someone who was otherwise insane.

When originally making enquiries, I learned from a document from the US authorities that Boston had once served in the US Coastguard. Today, coastguard training there is highly intensive and elements of it are at least as arduous for its recruits as many military training programs. What the level of training was that led to Boston becoming a member of the Coastguard at that time is not known but it follows that he must have received a considerable degree of training in order to join it. Whether that training involved knowledge of the process of drowning, including, for instance, how long it took for a drowning person to become unconscious and then die is not known. What seems fairly clear is that Boston may have had at least some knowledge of the process, as will become apparent later in this account. I learned that Boston was actually dismissed from the Coastguard service, due to his occasional inability to remain awake when on duty, the effects of alcohol being the suspected reason.

Charles Farmer at one point before my involvement, and during his own enquiries to try to trace the missing couple, had earlier written to the Police there. He asked for enquiries to be made to try to locate Christopher and Peta but received the astonishing reply that enquiries could be made if he first sent them a rather substantial sum of money. That, perhaps, says something about the state of affairs in that part of the world, leastwise at that time. Mr Farmer, desperate as he was, decided not to send any money.

It must be said that, at face value, the post mortem examination that took place on 10th July 1978, although concluding that Christopher and Peta had drowned, the resulting report did appear to fall rather short of the level of detail one would normally and routinely expect in Britain or the US, for example. The man who carried out the post mortem, Doctor Angel Maria Vasques Cuellar, who asserted in his report that his examination was made extremely difficult and was limited due to the state of decomposition that had actually worsened considerably in the two days since the 8th July when they were taken from the water. That was suggestive that the bodies were probably not refrigerated whilst awaiting the postmortems. There was no clear reference by the doctor to any specific injuries, marks or of the suggested bullet holes referred to by those involved in recovering the bodies. The doctor simply put all the 'injuries' or marks reported by others down to fish bites. He also made no attempt to estimate how long the bodies might have been in the water, even when I requested an estimate from him later. During my Police career, I have, through long Criminal Investigation experience, seen rather a lot of dead bodies, including ones in various stages of decomposition. Doctor Cuellar did not know of course that the pair were alive on 29th June, but it was rather obvious to me, let alone a medical expert, that the pair must have been murdered at least several days prior to the 8th July finding of the bodies, even taking account of the fact that decomposition would be faster in the warm waters in that part of the world, than in cooler waters elsewhere. It may be that Doctor Cuellar, aware that the bodies were bound and weighted when found, and had both drowned, murder being glaringly evident, there was little point in him doing more. That said, elsewhere, blood samples would have been taken as a matter of routine as it could not be assumed the pair had not been first drugged in some way, to enable them both to be tied up and thrown into the sea without a struggle.

It would probably only be a few hours sail from Hunting Cay to the location of Punta de Manabique and Peta, in her letter, referred to it as a likely easy sail with the wind behind them. It is logical to assume that, if stopping off at the Tres Puntas peninsular on the 29th June, possibly for another overnight stop, there would not be much reason to remain there for long the following day in such a remote area. Punta de Manabique is for a number of reasons now a protected area of considerable natural beauty. They could have stopped off there for that very reason, either at Boston's or their own suggestion but they were hardly equipped to explore the jungle-covered and swampy interior. It would not have normally taken more than around three hours to sail on from there across the Amatique Bay to Livingston. Peta had anyway indicated pretty clearly in her letter that she had had quite enough of sailing and was obviously keen to end it and get to Livingston, and from there catch a ferry boat to Puerto Cortez.

There was an assertion by Boston to Charles Farmer, in a transatlantic telephone call, during Mr Farmer's own enquiries before my involvement, that *The Justin B* had at some stage sustained a split mast. Boston said that was due to a storm but any such bad weather in that area was never confirmed and neither was it mentioned by Peta. But, after stopping off at Punta de Manabique, the location of the bodies, and then leaving there, where did Boston, his sons and *The Justin B* then go? There did emerge another story, in addition to the split mast one, and that was that *The Justin B* might have become disabled in that area, or was partly disabled due to engine trouble but that, again, was never confirmed either. In all probability, both stories were probably untrue. I anyway received an official meteorological report that there was no record of any storms in that area that reasonably could have accounted for *The Justin B* suffering a split mast. No engine trouble, mast damage or storm was mentioned by Peta in her letter, and one might think that any such events might have been mentioned by Peta, had they actually occurred. As things were to eventually turn out, the question of stories of a split mast or engine trouble was irrelevant to actual events.

I assumed that if Boston was the murderer, it is not very likely that he would have chosen to remain very long at or near the murder location. It was later discovered from a port record, that *The Justin B* did sail into Livingston on Thursday 6th July but contrary to an earlier customs document record in Dangriga, Belize, dated 26th June, that indicated five people were aboard prior to it leaving there for its originally intended destination of Puerto Cortes, that was not the case on 6th July when just Boston and his sons were aboard. Christopher and Peta had obviously been murdered several days prior to 6th July and their bodies were not to be found until the 8th. It was revealed, and can now be seen, that prior to setting out on their trip on *The Justin B*, Christopher and Peta were falsely shown, on the Dangriga Customs House document, as being members of *The Justin B's* crew, i.e. sailors, rather than the passengers they really were. Boston had lodged that document on 26th June, 1978, with the Customs authorities just two days before they sailed south in the direction of Placencia. Stating that Christopher and Peta were crew was nothing other than a simple ruse to hide the fact that Boston was not licensed to carry passengers on his boat. It is obvious that Customs did not consider questioning the fact that the small six-ton vessel needed so many people to crew it, including two young boys. Below are copies of the actual relevant port records of this, each bearing Boston's signature:

CREW LIST

Name	age	Nationality	Occupation
Duane Boston	37	American	Master
Chris Farmer —	25	British	Sailor
Peter Frampton —	24	British	Sailor
Vince Boston	13	American	Sailor
Russell Boston	12	American	Sailor

CAPTAIN.

**PORT RECORD OF CREW LIST
SIGNED BY BOSTON**

Agent's Name _____ Master

Port of Belize - Entry Outwards

No. 20/78

Rig ___ S/Aux, _____ Ship's Name ___ Justin 3,

If British, name of Port of her Registry	If Foreign, name of country to which she belongs	Tonnage	Number of Men	Master's Name	Port of Destination
BELIZE		6	4	DUANE BOSTON	PUERTO CORTES HONDURAS,

The Angelus Press

Date of Entry __26th June,__ 19 78

Master or Agent

FURTHER PORT RECORD SIGNED BY BOSTON

Reproduced below is a map I prepared of the area encompassing the relevant parts of Belize, Guatemala and Honduras. Shown is Placencia from where they set off at 7 am on the morning of 28th June. The location of Hunting Cay is also indicated, as is the originally intended destination of Puerto Cortes in Honduras that, in common with Belize, also borders with Guatemala. The Tres Puntas peninsular where Punta de Manabique is located is shown, as is the town of Livingston and adjacent Puerto Barrios, both across Amatique Bay from the peninsular. Punta de Manabique can be seen to lie on the southern tip of the peninsula which can be seen to be on a direct sea route from Hunting Cay to Livingston. It was obvious that Peta and Christopher did decide to take the lighthouse keeper's advice, and sailed on *The Justin B* for Livingston rather than the originally intended Puerto Cortes but were never to reach their destination. Indicated on the map is the place where their murdered bodies were found, part way along their route, and across the bay from Livingston. Also shown at the bottom left of the map is a small and remote inland town called El Estor evidently only easily accessible at the time by boat. The likely relevance of El Estor will shortly become clear.

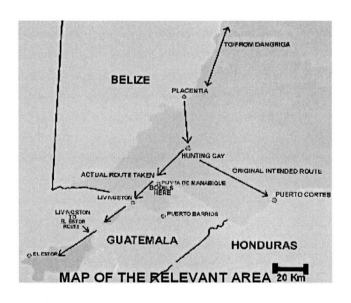

Chapter Four
The Investigation

As the murdered bound and weighted bodies were found in the sea, and held stationary at that spot by the weights, some 200 metres from the shore, they could only have been put there from a boat. The last known vessel they were known to have been on was, of course, Boston's, so he needed to be urgently traced with a view to him answering some questions. However, I still had to keep an open mind as to whether Boston was the murderer despite my strong suspicions. One reason for this was that it was difficult for me to imagine how he would have been able to kill a pretty fit young man like Christopher, without any sort of struggle involving a commotion and noise, and also kill Peta, both presumably within a short period of one another, and with his two sons on board at the time. After all, *The Justin B* was a quite small vessel. That was, of course, if the boys were actually on board at the time of the killings.

I tried to imagine various possible scenarios as to how the murders might have been committed on *The Justin B* without the boys knowing anything. I also wondered that if Boston had killed them, what could have been his motive? Was it for the money and personal items they possessed or could there have been a sexual motive involving Peta? Alternatively, had there perhaps been an argument and violent fight onboard involving Christopher and Boston, ending with Christopher being rendered unconscious, perhaps followed by Peta's murder as a result of her having been a witness? I could only ponder where Boston's sons could possibly have been at the time of the murders, if actually committed on *The Justin B.* I concluded that logically, the boys might have either been ashore at such a time or alternatively, had simply been fast asleep in their cabin if it had occurred at night. I simply could not imagine any other logical scenario. In the event, how completely wrong I was as to what had really happened.

It did appear, from what was learned, that Boston may have known that they possessed at least some money which seemingly was mostly in the form of Traveller's Cheques. That was because Charles Farmer in England, after managing to contact Boston's father, Russell Boston, did receive a return telephone call from Boston. That call took place on or about 25th January 1979 some six months after the bodies had actually been found, but of which fact Boston and Mr Farmer were then unaware of. Mr Farmer was at that time still trying to find out why his son and Peta had gone missing. During that conversation, Mr Farmer very sensibly did his best not to give any impression that he actually suspected Boston of having anything to do with his son's and Peta's disappearance. Ever the journalist, and despite his suspicions and inevitable stress, he had some specific questions he wanted to ask and he made careful notes of his questions and Boston's replies. Mr Farmer asked him if the couple were OK for money and Boston replied that "They seemed to be!" That reply was perhaps suggestive that he actually knew they were

OK for money. I wondered just how he might know that. I speculated that Christopher might have already handed over some money to Boston in payment for the trip on *The Justin B*, in which event Boston could possibly have seen where the money had been produced from and noted that there was more. A reply to Mr Farmer, to the effect, that he had no idea how they were for money might perhaps have been expected. On the other hand, I thought Boston could also simply have guessed that they were OK for money on the basis that he would know they could hardly travel without it, or simply that they had not given him any indication that they were short of funds.

Boston told Charles Farmer very clearly, when asked the specific question, that he "Dropped Christopher and Peta off" near Porto (Puerto) Barrios between 3 and 6 July. He also told Mr Farmer that he *guessed* he saw them boarding a ferry in Livingston around 9th July but when he went around he said they had gone. Boston also told Mr Farmer that he had charged the couple the sum of five hundred dollars for their time on the boat, a figure that Mr Farmer considered would have been wildly excessive. Mr Farmer was of the belief that at that time Christopher and Peta would probably have had of the order of five hundred to a maximum of one thousand pounds' worth of currency in their possession. Charging Christopher and Peta five hundred dollars would likely have relieved them of an enormous chunk, if not virtually all of their money. In the event, the reply by Boston to Charles Farmer, that the couple *seemed* to be OK for money might have been of some significance from what was eventually discovered. A copy of Mr Farmer's notes of his transatlantic telephone conversation with Boston is reproduced below. I should mention that the conversation is repeated within a copy of an important document that appears later in this account. Mr Farmer's own notes regarding his conversation with Boston were incorporated in the official Police witness statement I originally obtained from him, a photocopy of which was amongst all the other copy documents I had retained since:

Q. "Is that Duane Boston?"

A. "Yes".

Q. "The Mr Duane Boston, owner of *The Justin B*?"

A. "Yes, I was."

Q. "This is Charles Farmer, father of Dr Christopher Farmer who was on board your boat with Miss Frampton last year. I would like to ask you a few questions, as we have not heard from them since Hunting Cay, in June."

A. "Yes, I remember them. I spoke to someone from the British Consul and told them all about them."

Q. "Yes, quite, you landed them where?"

A. "Near Porto Barrios."

Q. "In Guatemala?"

A. "Yes, in Guatemala."

Q. "What sort of coast?"

A. "The beach."

Q. "How were they dressed?"

A. "I can't remember—jeans or something."

Q. "Had Chris got his medical bag?"

A. "His what?"

Q. "Well Chris was a medical doctor, and he was going to another medical appointment, he would have his medical bag."

A. "No. A duffle bag."

Q. "Were they alright for money?"

A. "They seemed to be alright."

Q. "Had they got their air tickets to the USA?"

A. "I wouldn't know."

Q. "Any idea where they might have stayed if not in hotels in Livingston?"

A. "I expect they caught a ferry."

Q. "Do you know who might have posted the letter on 18th July?"

A. "No."

Q. "Any mention of Chris going to Trinidad and Peta going to New Orleans?"

A. "Might have been mentioned in a discussion. They intended to sail to Costa Rica, but they were in no hurry."

Q. "We understand you had some trouble with the boat, it was damaged?"

A. "Yes, the mast was split.

Q. "Was it gale damage?"

A. "Yes."

Q. "Where was this?"

A. "Off Porto Barrios."

Q. "You were at Hunting Cay on 29th June, when did you drop them off, what date and when did you get to Livingston?"

A. "I dropped them off somewhere about the 3rd to the 6th July. I don't remember."

Q. "We have records showing you entered Livingston on the 6th."

A. "Don't remember, but if you say so."

Q. "Whereabout were you seen by fishermen?"

A. "I don't remember any fishermen."

Q. "Were there any drugs aboard the boat?"

A. "No."

Q. "Were they clear on their next destination?"

A. "They were travelling to Mexico, then changed to go to Costa Rica."

Q. "Do you still have the boat's log or any details of the trip?"

A. "No."

Q. "How would you expect them to get to Livingston?"

A. "Hire a Dhorry."

Q. "If they had gone through normal channels in Livingston, what problems would they have arriving in Honduras?"

A. "Everybody does it."

Q. "How would they get into Guatemala if no entry stamps on their passports?"

A. "No questions are asked."

Q. "Are there any Communist guerrillas in Guatemala?"

A. "I've not heard of any, but natives think there are."

Q. "Had they mentioned going to Peru or Colombia?"

A. "Just talk, and mention of San Andreas."

Q. "Did they pay for their time onboard?"

A. "Yes, 500 dollars." (I have enquired amongst friends and this is regarded as a ridiculously large figure, perhaps $50 each is more realistic. In fact, I calculate Peta and Chris could have had anything between £500 to £1000 in currency in their joint possession at this time).

Q. "What cargo did you pick up at Dangriga?"

A. "Did not have any cargo—only coconuts and mangoes for ballast."

Q. "Have you any idea what might have happened to them?"

A. "No."

Q. "There is no trace of them ever having been in Livingston, except your report of seeing them on a ferry."

A. "Oh—I guess I saw them around the 9th boarding a ferry, but when I had walked round they had gone. Let me know if you hear anything about them."

As Boston and his sons were the last known people to have been in the company of Peta and Christopher, not only did he need to be seen by the Police, but his two young sons Vince and Russell obviously needed to be interviewed too. The boys, said to be aged respectively 13 and 12 years at the time, must have been enjoying something of an extended adventure holiday. Quite some time had since passed and both boys in my view were anyway each of the age to doubtless be able to recall a good deal about various events during that time. That, I assumed, must have included the period of time that Christopher and Peta were aboard *The Justin B.* Just why the two boys were in Central America with Boston, and not at home in America where their sister and the third brother were, was not known.

Boston, it was discovered, at some point after Christopher's and Peta's disappearance, had a conversation with the owner of a small hotel in Livingston about them. That hotel, which still exists, is called The Casa Rosada and the owner at that time was a Mrs Jean Swanson. Mrs Swanson's conversation with him came to light during requested enquiries being made by a British FCO official when originally trying to trace the missing pair. Hotels were very obvious places to make some enquiries. It emerged that Mrs Swanson was somehow aware that the couple had been in Placencia at some point in time although she most probably only learned that from Boston. Mrs Swanson actually said that Boston had told her he had put Christopher and Peta ashore at Stann Creek, Placencia which is, of course, the place they set off from on 29th June intending to head for Puerto Cortes. Whether what could be concluded to mean is that they had disembarked from *The Justin B* at Placencia and then re-embarked for the trip to Puerto Cortes is unknown. Boston though, further told her that he *thought* he saw them both boarding a ferry at Livingston around the second week of July, 1978, but adding he "couldn't be sure." That latter assertion is, of course, a repeat of what he had also told Charles Farmer, having also made the same assertion to a British Consul official in San Francisco during earlier enquiries. Of course, he could not have seen them there at all because they were then dead. However, Boston could not then have known that the bodies had actually been found on 8th July. He was to be told of this very much later and no doubt would have been left deeply shocked as a result.

His assertion to Mrs Swanson and the others had clearly given the completely false impression at that time that they were alive and well during the early part of July. Mrs Swanson repeated her account of what Boston had told her when later questioned again during continuing enquiries. Had the bodies never been found, which was obviously the murderer's intention, then the myth about them being alive, at least up to 18th July 1978 when Peta's letter was postmarked, would undoubtedly have persisted indefinitely.

The FCO wrote to Mr Farmer on 29th November 1978 and below is an extract from that letter which outlines Boston's assertions to one of their officials after he was traced:

Our Consulate-General in San Francisco spoke to Mr Duane Boston by telephone on 30 October. The address through which they contacted him, which we assume remains the same, is as given in my letter to you of 17 October: Box 134, Smith's Flat, California 95222. Duane Boston said that he remembered Chris and Peter very well and that they had been frequent passengers on his boat. He said that he agreed to take them from Belize to Puerto Cortes. Stops were made at various islands but as the Justin B subsequently required repairs the two passengers disembarked at a peninsula across the bay from Livingston. It appears that their intention was to hire a native boat. Boston added that he thought he saw them in Livingston boarding a ferry during the second week in July but cannot be sure. He did not really know their ultimate destination but said they could be heading for San Andreas Island or Trinidad or that they might go to Colombia or Peru.

On 15th December 1978 the FCO wrote a further letter to Mr Farmer, and what follows is an extract from that letter:

Dear Mr. Farmer,

Thank you for your letter of 3 December. You may like to know that our Consul in San Francisco recently arranged to meet Mr Boston to find out whether he could in any way amplify the details he had already provided about Peter and Christopher's departure from his boat.

I am afraid, however, that Mr Boston was able to add very little to what has already been reported. He said that the couple were dropped off on the peninsula of Tres Puntas. He was not sure of the exact date but said it would be between 3 - 6 July. At that time the boat was sailing from the Spadella Islands in the Gulf of Honduras to have a split mast repaired in Livingston. When he dropped them off Boston assumed that they intended to take a native boat to Puerto Barrios. However, he thought he saw them in Livingston a few days later boarding a ferry bound for Puerto Barrios. We understand that anyone dropped off on the coast above Livingston can easily walk down the beach into Livingston without passing through immigration control and a twice-daily ferry runs between Livingston and Puerto Barrios. Passengers on the ferry are not subject to immigration control and tickets are not issued by name.

I speculated that if *Boston* was the killer, logically he might have been expected to have murdered Christopher and

Peta during the hours of darkness, rather than in broad daylight, and more likely than not, at a time when his two sons were asleep in their cabin. If Peta was asleep in her cabin, I thought that perhaps he could have quickly surprised and incapacitated Christopher, possibly by striking him on the head from behind and then, whilst Christopher was stunned, binding his hands, legs and feet, attaching him to a weight and then putting him over the side. I thought that if that was the case, then it would logically have involved some prior planning and also a degree of preparation regarding timing, a weapon to use, ropes and a suitable weight. I thought it possible that he might then have gone to the small galley cabin, where Christopher and Peta had their bunks, and quickly overpowered Peta, silenced and bound her, attached her to some weight, and put her over the side of the vessel to drown with Christopher. I thought such a scenario could have happened without the two boys being aware of it, and certainly if very little noise was involved. Alternatively, something similar could have happened if the boys were for some reason not on the boat at the time, maybe even having been sent ashore on some pretext, albeit I thought this would not be likely at night. It did also occur to me that if the British couple were aboard the vessel when the two boys went to their cabin for the night, or alternatively, returned from some absence from the boat, just what could Boston have told them to account for the fact that the couple were no longer present?

Whatever had happened, in terms of exactly when, how and why the murders were committed, and whether Boston was indeed the murderer was obviously more than just a little difficult for myself to finally resolve back in England. I was thousands of miles away from the scene of the murders and places where further enquiries were needed. The murders were committed within Guatemalan territory, quite possibly or probably by an American, and on what would then be deemed to be an American vessel if he owned it. The British Police anyway had no legal jurisdiction whatever to prosecute in the case and the fact that the victims were British was irrelevant. In the absence of any interest or involvement by the Guatemalan Police, the only Law Enforcement Agency with probable jurisdiction and in a position to investigate further appeared to be in the United States of America. The only avenue for the case to be taken forward, was for me to prepare a comprehensive report of all the known facts, and to send it, with copy documents, to the US authorities, which I did. My report was dated 30th August 1979.

I requested that the US Law Enforcement Authorities make further enquiries with a view to them bringing the murderer to justice in an American court. I had finally come to the inescapable view that Boston was indeed the murderer and I believed there was a very urgent need for the investigation to be continued in the US. Indeed, I believed there was sufficient circumstantial evidence already available to enable Boston to be arrested. His sons, over a year on since the murders, could also be interviewed.

Throughout my own involvement, I had maintained regular communication with the victim's families, principally via Charles Farmer. Not long after my report was sent off to the US, I was assigned to take temporary charge of the Special Branch Unit at Manchester International Airport. On my return to the Special Branch office at police headquarters some two years later, I looked at the main file in the administration department to see if there had been any developments in the US. I discovered a further document had been inserted into the file. That showed that Boston, during my absence, had been traced and interviewed by a Sergeant Kelly of the San Rafael Police Department who had then sent a copy of his report to the GMP. The report was dated 5th March 1981, a little short of three years after the murders. I, of course, photocopied that report too. What might have happened subsequent to Sergeant Kelly's interview with Boston is not known at all, other than that he did write to Charles Farmer in response to a letter to him from Mr Farmer. Page one of Kelly's 5th March report was somehow separated and lost but copies of the 2nd and 3rd pages of it, in the event the most relevant, and addressed to someone called Miller, who I assumed to be his senior officer, are reproduced below:

When asked to relate the series of events regarding his contact with Mr. Farmer and Miss Frampton, Boston's memory of the exact dates and times was extremely vague.

Boston stated that to the best of his recollection he first met Mr. Farmer and Miss Frampton at a hotel in Belize in the country of Belize. He stated that at that time he took them on as passengers on his boat and had intended to head for Port of Cortez. Along with Mr. Farmer and Miss Frampton was Boston's sons, Vince and Russell, and he had picked up an additional passenger who had also been at the hotel in Belize, whom he only knew as Sharon. He described Sharon as a tall blonde female in her mid-twenties who was from the State of Missouri in the United States. He further stated that at the time he met them and also during the trip that Miss Frampton was drinking a great deal of alcohol. He also stated that Mr. Farmer was shooting some type of drugs into his arm with a needle. He stated he did not know what these drugs were. He also stated that Miss Frampton and the third passenger, Sharon, were arguing a great deal throughout the trip.

They sailed for about two days and went to Corzal in Belize. Afterwhich they turned around and went back to Kaycocker where the third passenger, Sharon, disembarked and did not return to the boat. They then left Kaycocker and went to Belize where they obtained shipping papers and began to head for Port of Cortez. They next stopped at Huntingkay where they stopped for a short time and then once again began to head for Port of Cortez. Due to bad weather, Boston stated that they tied their boat up at a point somewhere between Huntingkay and Port of Cortez. While waiting for the weather to clear, Boston stated that two male subjects, whom he described as natives, came by in another boat heading towards Port of Barrios. Boston stated that Mr. Farmer and Miss Frampton then disembarked from his boat and went on this other boat as it would be easier for them to reach their destination, via Port of Barrios.

Boston stated that after that incident he believed he went to Astar for approximately two weeks after which he went to Livingston. The only date that Boston could positively remember was July 16th, as he stated he called his girlfriend from that location on approximately July 16th or 17th. He stated he remembered this date because he was calling his daughter due to the fact that it was her birthday, which is July 16th. He stated that at the time he was in Livingston

PAGE 2 OF SERGEANT KELLY'S REPORT

on approximately July 16th he thought he saw Mr. Farmer and Miss Frampton at that time.

It's interesting to note that the last letter from Miss Frampton is postmarked Livingston, Guatemala, 16th July 1978. Due to this information I asked Boston if he had mailed any letters for Miss Frampton or any one else to which he replied no that he had not.

Boston stated that he had no idea who could've committed the murders, however he stated that this type of violent death is very common for that area. He stated that during his time down there, he had seen numerous acts of violence which appeared to him to be a way of life for the people of that area.

Boston could relate no further pertinent information to this case. In regards to you inquiry as to his background, Boston has an extensive record dating back to 1961. He's been arrested for disturbing the peace, assault, burglary (several counts), possession of stolen property, carrying a concealed firearm, and rape. It is also my understanding that Mr. Boston was a main suspect in a homicide investigation in the city of Sacramento, California, approximately thirteen years ago. This investigation extended from the disappearance of his second wife who has never been found.

Boston is presently out on bail pending charges on our case and will be making additional court appearances in the very near future.

If I can be of any additional assistance in the future, please don't hestiate to contact me.

Sincerely,

James R. Kelly

JAMES R. KELLY, SERGEANT
San Rafael Police Department

PAGE THREE OF SERGEANT KELLY'S REPORT

That interview, as can be seen, took place on 5th, March 1981 but the result was, to my mind, disappointing. It was very obvious that the case needed to be progressed very much further and with some evidence of determination. The tone of the questioning, from Kelly's report, had the appearance of being rather less than *robust*. It seemed to give the impression that Boston was being treated by Kelly more like a possible witness, rather than the extremely strong murder suspect that he clearly was in the original report I had sent to the US. That said, it may have been that the interview tone was deliberately intended to be a preliminary move by Kelly to test Boston's reaction and responses, with further enquiries to follow being the intention. It will be noted that Kelly mistakenly referred to the postmark on the envelope of Peta's last letter as being 16th July, rather than the 18th.

It was my firm expectation at the time that further enquiries subsequent to Kelly's report would be made. There was no mention of Vince or Russell Boston, by then getting on for the better part of three years older than at the time of the murders, having been interviewed up to 5th March 1981, or of there being any intention that they would be. I guessed, completely wrongly in the event, that those interviews would naturally follow as a matter of routine. However, what I thought should have happened in the investigation was somewhat irrelevant because the plain fact was that the case was the entire responsibility of US Law Enforcement. This, however, did nothing to lessen my own feelings of frustration and helplessness at not being able to achieve more in a practical way. There was absolutely nothing further the British Police could do. The documents sent to the US made it perfectly obvious what was required of Law Enforcement there and it was hardly necessary, or acceptable, for the British Police, or me in particular, to try to tell the American authorities how to go about a murder investigation. What had also troubled me was that Kelly's interview gave me the impression that he was questioning Boston on behalf of the

British Police rather than US law enforcement and his report that was sent to England ended, "…if I can be of any additional assistance in the future, please don't hesitate to contact me!" This seemed to illustrate fairly clearly that the question of jurisdiction had not at all been understood by Sgt Kelly, or the officer (Miller) to whom his report was initially directed to.

What did firmly emerge from Sergeant Kelly's interview, though, was that Boston had asserted that, at the Tres Puntas peninsular, he had offloaded Christopher and Peta from *The Justin B* to two *natives* crewing another boat, in order for them, as Boston put it, "to continue their journey." Of course, it was impossible to miss that he had previously said to one person that he dropped them off at the peninsular and to another that he did so as they had the intention of then hiring a native boat. Additionally, and in my view, of prospectively crucial importance, was that Boston categorically stated to Sergeant Kelly that he was in Livingston on 16th or 17th July as he made a telephone call from there to the US, it being his daughter's birthday on 16th. Peta's last letter, as we know, was postmarked Livingston on the 18th July, only one or perhaps two days after Boston confessed to being definitely present there. My own very firm belief was that he was still there on 18th and that he posted Peta's letter, having deliberately kept possession of it for over two weeks after having committed the murders. I could still only wonder just where Boston and his sons had been during several days when the whereabouts of *The Justin B* were not known. There was an official port report clearly indicating that *The Justin B* had sailed into Livingston on 6th July 1978 but no records were produced revealing when it actually left there. Nothing at all was known about *The Justin B's* movements between the 29th June up to the 6th July, other than that, it had stopped at the peninsular most probably later on the 29th and perhaps part of 30th June. There was a similar mystery for the period between 6th July and 16th/17th July when on the latter date(s) Boston said he was definitely in Livingston from where he made his phone call to the US.

Boston's assertion to Sgt Kelly, of handing the pair over to two natives passing in another boat at the peninsular, was in very serious conflict indeed with the differing accounts he had previously made to Charles Farmer and two British officials, as to the exact circumstance of him parting company with Christopher and Peta. It seems that Boston never considered the possibility of his differing accounts to different people being compared. Which of his stories were to be believed? More to the point, were any of them true? Boston's accounts, realistically, ought not to have differed to the degrees they did and so I did not believe any of them. To my mind, he would have been better to have stuck to just one story.

In a personal letter dated 4th June 1981, Charles Farmer, Christopher's father, wrote to Sergeant Kelly of the San Rafael Police Department in California. That was almost certainly because he wanted to encourage enquiries there, by reiterating Boston's conflicting accounts that were anyway highlighted in my original report to the US. Mr Farmer advised Kelly that Boston had very clearly told him over the telephone that he had put the missing couple (ashore) about two miles from a place called Porto (Puerto) Barrios so that they could walk into town, presumably meaning Puerto Barrios itself rather than Livingston. Puerto Barrios is situated some 8 or 10 miles to the east of Livingston but there is a very wide river estuary to the sea between Puerto Barrios and Livingston. The two towns, being several miles apart, meant that Christopher and Peta, had they really been dropped near Puerto Barrios, would have been faced with a very difficult long trek westward along the coast towards Livingston. But they could hardly walk across that approximate mile wide estuary of the Rio Dulce to get to Livingston on the other side so a boat would have been necessary to make such a crossing. Livingston was anyway where they wanted to go to catch a ferry to Puerto Cortes so why would they, as Boston had claimed, in one story at least, be dropped several miles away from Livingston near Puerto Barrios instead? Boston, in an interview with a British consul, had conversely declared that he had put them ashore at a location near Livingston whereas he told another he had dropped them at a peninsular which could only be Tres Puntas. A Council official had at the time expressed considerable doubt about one of Boston's assertions for the simple reason that he knew the jungle at that particular location grew right down to the edge of the sea with no access roads along the coast in either direction.

In due course though, I ended my tour of duty with Special Branch and returned to normal Operational Criminal Investigation work in Manchester, then serving respectively at two other busy Sub Divisional Headquarters before I finally retired in April 1987, after 30 years of service. I, then, became chief of security at a large British national company and then retired again a little over six years later. I still had a need to keep busy though and this resulted in me becoming a volunteer driver with my County's Ambulance Service, this keeping me well occupied for some 14 more years.

Coincidentally, I learned very much later that Boston had for a time worked for an Ambulance Service.

It has to be said that since my active involvement in this murder case ended, and during the years following my retirement from the Police, I occasionally wondered about how things might, or might not, have progressed in the US regarding the murders. Since I had heard nothing, and there was no obligation for anyone to keep me informed anyway, that is unless I was needed as a witness, I wondered what might have eventually transpired. I knew Boston had a bad criminal record and Sergeant Kelly's report referred to Boston having convictions for, several counts of burglary, disturbing the peace, assault, rape, possession of stolen property and carrying a concealed firearm, those offences going back to 1961. I wondered if Boston, with such a record, might have subsequently been arrested and jailed for some other serious crime or crimes in America. I knew from a report I had received from the US via Interpol that Boston was at that time wanted for other alleged offences over there. If Boston had subsequently been convicted of some very serious US offence(s), a very long, perhaps even a life prison sentence could have resulted. Such an event, I thought, might perhaps have caused the American authorities to conclude there was little point in pursuing him further for the murders in Guatemala. Alternatively, could Boston have possibly been arrested, tried, convicted and imprisoned for the murders in Guatemala and I had simply never been told? That could have happened if, following arrest, he had pleaded guilty which would have meant I was not required to attend as a witness. I still harboured another worrying possibility though. Had the case been neglected and allowed to go cold?

Whatever I thought could or should have happened regarding the US investigation into the murders of Christopher and Peta, there was a very good reason why I had never heard anything further, in terms of a positive result or otherwise. That was because the original investigation in America may have been badly handled, quite possibly lacking essential proper supervision and direction. The case, despite its gravity, had indeed just been allowed to *stall* and then go cold as I had feared. It seemed clear to me then, and now, that this dreadful crime had simply never been enthusiastically progressed further all those years ago despite Boston, apparently having been interviewed, and then apparently sought for an interview on a second occasion. I did learn at one stage that a lawyer, on Boston's behalf, was reported to have complained that Boston was being harassed by the Police. Whether that complaint might have deterred the Police from pressing on with the enquiries can only be guessed at. I was deeply unhappy to eventually learn that neither of his sons had ever been interviewed and I remain astonished why this very obvious step was never taken. Certainly, to interview them when their father was actually a suspect, assuming they were living with him, might have presented something of a problem, albeit not necessarily an insurmountable one. However, that is something I will turn to later in this account. The plain fact was that Boston, for whatever reason, was never arrested or charged. During the years that followed, my mind occasionally and inevitably went back to the case. For me, it always represented very seriously unfinished business. Detectives, including retired ones, do not like knowing that any murderer has escaped justice and remains free. Some people will conclude that the US abjectly failed in their original investigation and one evening many years later, in 2017, I was to get the distinct impression that this is now viewed with at least a little level of embarrassment by some people in the US.

I should mention that very soon after seeing Sgt Kelly's report, and just before being transferred back to Operational Criminal Investigation work, I had gone to see the (new) chief of my department. I pointed out that as I was leaving, someone ought to be designated to "keep an eye" on the case despite it being in American hands. The response I got was a positive one, in that I was told someone would do that. Had I remained in the department I could never have been content to know, believe or accept that this dreadful case had just stalled and gone cold over in the US. And so, just prior to leaving the department, I was left under the clear understanding that any follow-up contact thought necessary, to try to "encourage" determined action in the US, and keep the families updated, would be done by my successor or someone else. I can only presume it never happened though. Indeed, I am fairly confident that after I left there was no further communication whatever, one way or the other, between the GMP and the US authorities. Knowing Charles Farmer as well as I did though, I am surprised that he would not have at some stage made his feelings very well known when and if he came to perceive that nothing seemed to be happening in the US. If he did, I have no way of knowing. But that is now all in the distant past and there is little point in recriminations for events so many years ago. It was not to be until late 2015 that Penny Farmer and her mother Audrey were to have a discussion that decided them to raise the whole issue again with the GMP that did finally provide the initial trigger to get things moving again, thanks to Audrey still remembering my name. But I should add at this point that sometime earlier, actually around 2013, and unknown to anyone in England, the case in the US, although originally cold, had become not quite so cold as before. That is because I was eventually to learn that a certain Sergeant Robert (Bob) McCloskey of the Sacramento Police Department Cold Case Unit had decided to have a serious look into the possibility that Boston had not only murdered Christopher and Peta in 1978 but had also killed his wife Mary Lou ten years earlier in 1968. McCloskey had been involved from the start in what had been a missing person enquiry related to Mary Lou Boston who had disappeared, albeit in somewhat suspicious circumstances.

There is not the slightest room for doubt that one of Boston's sons, Vince, had for a long time been trying to persuade the US Police Authorities, even pestering, some thought, to investigate the case of his missing mother. He claimed he knew she had been murdered by Boston in 1968. He had also asserted to the Police that he had actually witnessed and had described the murders of Christopher and Peta by his father in 1978. Added to that, it is clear that Mary Lou's own parents were very suspicious about her disappearance and had made their own suspicions very well known to the Police, as had Mary Lou's younger brother. Originally Vince's claims and assertions were either deemed possibly too fanciful and not sufficiently reliable, or they felt there was just insufficient evidence other than Vince's say so. However, it seems that Bob McCloskey was not quite so sure and he was compelled to take Vince Boston's assertions very much more seriously. As a consequence, during a period as recently up to and including 2013, McCloskey had a great deal of contact with Vince Boston and simultaneously was reviewing everything known concerning the disappearance of Vince's mother. His enquiries went to the extent of communicating with Interpol and also the Belizean authorities about the murders of Christopher and Peta. That contact revealed for the first time a small piece of information, or leastwise an assertion, that Boston had actually been detained by the Belize authorities sometime after the bodies had been discovered. If true, that could only have been because he was viewed as a possible suspect for the murders. Any such detention in Belize could of course only have been the result of some prior information from Guatemala. Whether that communication originated from the Guatemalan Justice of the Peace who had summoned the Bomberos to recover the bodies, or possibly the Police or the Port Authorities there, is just not known. It seems, if what Bob McCloskey was told was correct, i.e. that Boston was detained, however briefly, in Belize on his arrival there after sailing from Guatemala, that detention would probably have been at Dangriga on 9th August 1978 shortly before Boston is known to have sold *The Justin B* at Sarteneja later that same month, apparently to an unknown American couple. So, contrary to what had previously been believed, the Police in Guatemala and or Belize may, after all, have been involved in some level of enquiries into the murders. Logically it would have been the Belize Port authorities, and perhaps other ports who would have been on the lookout for the arrival of *The Justin B*. They then, possibly by prior arrangement might have told the Police. Whether it was the port authorities and not the Police who detained Boston, assuming they had powers to detain and also deport, is not known. They most probably did have such powers in order to control people entering and leaving the country, but Boston would have to have told a story to whoever detained him, that could not be disproved. Therefore, in the absence of any other evidence, he was, according to what Bob McCloskey was told, simply deported to the US. What form that deportation took is not known, i.e. was he just told to leave Belize, or taken to the Border, or what? The Belize detention story was understood to have originated from a still serving (or retired) Senior Belizean Police officer who claimed to have some recollection of the case. Despite that story of Boston's detention, it transpired that neither Vince Boston nor his younger brother Russell, have any recollection at all of any such thing having happened which seems strange. It could be though that any such *detention* might have only been very brief, really only amounting to a stop check to answer some questions, after which he might have just been told to leave Belize.

Sergeant McCloskey, in 2013, had been very determined to try to get to the bottom of things and was seeking essential old documentation. He was dismayed to be advised that there had subsequently, but on an undisclosed date, been a very serious fire in a Belize judicial building in which all records, including those relating to Boston's alleged detention, had been destroyed. All the lost records were said to have been handwritten. How the unknown senior Belizean police officer knew or claimed to know something about Boston's apparent detention and deportation back in 1978 is unknown.

By 2013 it appeared that no other copies of anything relevant still existed anywhere so, at that stage, Bob McCloskey seemed firmly stuck. If only he could have known what lay at the bottom of a cardboard box in a garden shed in England! He didn't, and so, for a little while longer, things remained that way. Amy Crosby then joined the Sacramento Cold Case Unit and closely studied details that were known about both cases, having picked up where McCloskey had left off. But she too did not have any badly needed documents, specifically those involving the murders of Christopher and Peta so she appeared not to be able to make any further progress.

I was initially surprised and deeply intrigued to know just how Bob McCloskey and later Amy Crosby could, that is in 2013, possibly have had any knowledge at all about the murders of the British couple in 1978. They did, of course, know all about Mary Lou's disappearance in 1968 because they still had the missing file on that. That file indicated that quite exhaustive enquiries had been made to try to discover what had happened to Mary Lou, and also included the fact that she might have been a homicide victim who might well have been killed by Boston. My own original report and copy documents sent to the US, concerning the murders of Christopher and Peta, did touch upon Mary Lou's suspicious disappearance, but clearly no longer existed in the US, in common with the original GMP file. So how could Bob McCloskey and Amy Crosby possibly then have had any knowledge at all of the murders in Guatemala? The answer, in common with much about this case, also came as a huge surprise when I heard that Vince Boston had actually told them about it. At that time, had Bob McCloskey contacted the UK to ask for any information, which did not happen anyway, the GMP, like Michaela Clinch later in 2015, would have been unable to locate the original file and no one then serving in

GMP would have known anything at all about the case, nor who had dealt with it.

Chapter Five
The Fresh Look

I was involved in very many criminal cases during my long Police career but I never forgot about the awful circumstances of the murders of Christopher Farmer and Peta Frampton. I was occasionally conscious of their sad remains lying virtually forgotten in their adjacent simple graves in Puerto Barrios cemetery during the many years that followed. I never forgot the sketch of the gravesites made by Doctor Reyes either. Police officers, in common with journalists and lawyers usually develop their own *defence mechanisms* when dealing with some awful gut-wrenching cases they are involved in. That is to try to guard against becoming too much involved and personally affected by the horrors. Although I generally succeeded extremely well in that regard, the dreadful killings of Christopher and Peta did get to me somewhat and I had desperately wanted to see their killer apprehended. It was indeed very seriously unfinished business and a grossly unsatisfactory situation for their bereaved families too. I was particularly unhappy with that latter thought. I know I could not have done more myself but I had played a big part in it all and had at least discovered what had happened to them. I felt the families had, for whatever reason, been badly let down, and thought that it should never have been the case. On an odd occasion, I recalled that I still possessed my old working copy of the case documents. It had also crossed my mind, more than once, to possibly write a book broadly based on the facts of the case, for which the documents I had would assist in building a semi-fictional story. However, as well as changing all the names, I would have to invent a more *satisfactory* ending to that which pertained. I thought such an ending could perhaps be based on new scientific developments or imaginary unexpected fresh evidence coming to light years after the crime, as has often happened in some re-investigated old cold cases. That way, it could almost be imagined that the murderer was finally to pay for his crime.

As I indicated earlier in this book, the old thick file of damp and stained copy documents I had kept all those years that contained all the known facts of the case, was suddenly seen as being of prospective massive importance. They were brought out of their own long retirement and handed over to Detective Michaela Clinch of the GMP Cold Case Unit. Back in her office, she and her Department Chief Martin Bottomley, himself a senior retired GMP detective, reviewed and considered all the information in the file, just as I had done those many years before. The whole case, from that point on, could consequently be given a fresh look, the very reason that Police Cold Case units exist. Whether such a fresh look might lead to anything that could result in the murderer being arrested was quite something else. I was soon to learn that Detective Clinch and Martin Bottomley came to share my own original and long-held views. That surprised me not at all. A positive decision was arrived at and GMP established contact with US Law Enforcement authorities in Sacramento in California. That resulted in all the documents I had supplied, with a new GMP comprehensive covering report, being sent to the United States of America in the hope that the case might be re-opened over there for a completely new re-investigation, effectively starting from scratch. I was, to say the least, somewhat excited at the prospect, but was Silas Duane Boston still alive to warrant an investigation?

Some days after my papers had been handed over to Detective Clinch, my wife Jane, who naturally knew the main details about the case, decided on a whim, to do a bit of detective work herself. She Googled the name Silas Duane Boston on her iPad. She got a single hit immediately and it was a 2nd May 2005 post from a man called Vince Boston. He was asking in it for any information about his mother Mary Lou Boston, the wife of Silas Duane Boston. A copy of that post is reproduced below, followed by a photograph of a very attractive Mary Lou Boston:

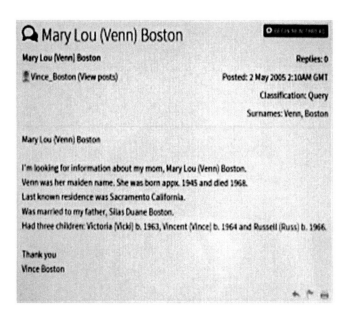

Mary Lou (Venn) Boston

Mary Lou (Venn) Boston   Replies: 0

Vince_Boston (View posts)   Posted: 2 May 2005 2:10AM GMT

                                                  Classification: Query

                                                  Surnames: Venn, Boston

Mary Lou (Venn) Boston

I'm looking for information about my mom, Mary Lou (Venn) Boston.
Venn was her maiden name. She was born appx. 1945 and died 1968.
Last known residence was Sacramento California.
Was married to my father, Silas Duane Boston.
Had three children: Victoria (Vicki) b. 1963, Vincent (Vince) b. 1964 and Russell (Russ) b. 1966.

Thank you
Vince Boston

VINCE BOSTON'S INTERNET POST

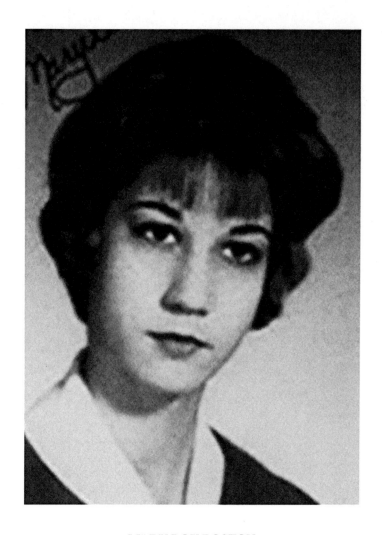

MARY LOU BOSTON

My wife, on reading Vincent Boston's post, said, "Oh, I think you had better read this," and passed me her iPad. Still the detective, despite being long retired, I at once noticed something that struck me as very odd indeed. It wasn't so much just my wondering just why Vince Boston, suddenly in 2005, had been moved to ask for "information about his mother" who had apparently just *disappeared* in 1968 so many years earlier. What was to me very strange was that Vince Boston stated that his mother had *died* in that year. How could he possibly know she had died when she had simply been reported missing to the Police, I had presumed by her husband Silas Duane Boston? I could not but get the distinct impression that Vince Boston was possibly a very troubled man and that he either suspected or maybe somehow knew something about his mother's disappearance and apparent death. I thought his post was a cry for help and when I read it I just said aloud, "Bloody Hell!"

Just what it could be, I thought, that was actually troubling Vince Boston sufficient to trigger that internet post so many years after his mother disappeared, and when he was just a very small boy. I, of course, copied the post and sent it to Detective Clinch who in turn advised her counterparts in the US about what was certainly an intriguing revelation. I thought my wife's little bit of detective work might be more than something of just interest. I thought at the time that her discovery might possibly prove to be of some assistance to the hoped-for new US investigation, particularly insofar as how interviews of Vince and Russell Boston might be approached. I speculated that if Vince Boston did actually know or suspect that his mother might have been murdered, and maybe actually suspected his own father of the killing, then he might be persuaded to reveal the reasons for his suspicions. It occurred to me that, on being interviewed, if it emerged that Vince did indeed suspect, or somehow knew his father had murdered his mother, he might just also have something useful to offer relative the murders of Christopher and Peta. So, I wondered if Vince Boston's internet post was prospectively a small key that might help open some long-locked doors? Sergeant Kelly's report made it clear that there had been suspicions that Mary Lou's disappearance had been regarded as a possible homicide, with Silas Duane Boston having been suspected of killing her.

Chapter Six
The Sacramento Police and the FBI

Detective Amy Crosby had transferred into the Sacramento Cold Case Unit in 2012. She would quickly have learned, if she had already not known, that Sergeant Bob McCloskey had been looking into the case concerning Mary Lou Boston and also that he somehow knew about the murders of Christopher Farmer and Peta Frampton despite the unavailability of my original report. Astonishingly, those two old cases being looked at, initially by McCloskey and later by Detective Crosby, were not very long afterwards to coincide with a most fortuitous event that was to take place in England in 2015. That event was, of course, when Christopher Farmer's sister Penny had asked the GMP to look again at the murder case involving her brother and Peta. To my mind, that was indeed another somewhat spooky coincidence coming at the particular time it did.

When Amy Crosby of The SPD Cold Case department, out of the blue in 2015, suddenly found herself presented with all the copy documents I had handed to the GMP, she must have been astonished almost beyond words. And at the same time somewhat overjoyed. She, along with her partner Detective Janine LeRose, then set about reviewing all those documents and comparing and combining the various elements of critical information in them with whatever it was they already knew or suspected. After doing so they too could do nothing other than coming to the same inescapable conclusions as Michaela Clinch and Martin Bottomley in Manchester, and myself. However, I did not then know just what information or suspicions they already had about the murders of Christopher and Peta. Indeed, I did not know how they could at that time possibly know anything about the murders in Guatemala at all. Nor quite what they knew or suspected about Mary Lou's disappearance. The SPD anyway decided that they needed to seek advice from the Federal Bureau of Investigation (FBI) as to just how they might be able to proceed with such an old case of a double murder committed in Guatemala. That is if they could actually proceed at all.

As a result, they entered into consultation with officers of the FBI who were also based at Sacramento, including FBI Special Agent David Sesma. Attorneys in Sacramento were also involved and consulted, including particularly the critical question of jurisdiction in the murders of Christopher and Peta. It was finally decided, after some further enquiries about Boston's citizenship and ownership of *The Justin B*, that the US did indeed have jurisdiction to deal with the matter. And so it was that all working together, the Sacramento Police, the FBI and a team of attorneys set about re-investigating the whole case. This time, however, with considerably more enthusiasm than was evident all those years earlier when all the evidence had been fresh, original documents existed and all prospective witnesses were still alive with their individual fresh memories. Also, when Boston was very much younger.

The old copy documents the GMP had sent to Sacramento, effectively, comprised pretty well everything that the US needed in order to finally set things in motion.

In the latter part of 2016, a year after I handed over all the documents to Detective Clinch, she received some news from Sacramento concerning what was still an ongoing and very active investigation into the murders in Guatemala. As a result, she telephoned me again. I wondered, having heard nothing for a year, if I was going to be told bad news so I at once asked her if the US authorities had decided to finally *pull the plug* on the case. Her news, however, was completely to the contrary. She told me that the US Authorities, comprising the Sacramento Police, the FBI and a team of US Attorneys had made what she then termed, and rather understated, as 'considerable progress' with the re-opened investigation. Not only that, but they had also reached the point, I was told, when they shortly afterwards intended to arrest Silas Duane Boston, who was still alive, with a view to him being indicted for the 1978 murders of Christopher Farmer and Peta Frampton. I was told that the families had been informed. That news of Boston's impending arrest absolutely made my day. I was totally and utterly elated almost beyond words and felt the hairs at the back of my neck rise and I got gooseflesh on my arms. When I think about it, I still feel euphoric. It was fantastic news.

I, of course, desperately wished to know just what 'considerable progress' and possible further evidence had been obtained to justify Boston's impending arrest. However, Detective Clinch told me that at that time she had specifically been asked by the US authorities not to disclose to anyone whatever it was that she had been told. I must say that I inwardly felt distinctly piqued, indeed quite annoyed at this as I was undeniably rather more than just a minor cog in the whole matter, having been the original investigator. Despite being retired, I thought I might have been unquestionably considered to still be a party to the investigation as a whole. I would like to think that the US did not really mean that I should be excluded as to the specific progress that had been made but I did not press the matter with Michaela. Having waited the better part of 40 years, I had to be content to be patient for a little longer and I did not say to her what I actually thought about being effectively excluded from the loop. After all, I had provided the means from which everything else had finally followed on. In the meantime, I could only speculate as to what developments could possibly have emerged from the further enquiries in America that finally led to Boston's impending arrest. In the event, I could never have begun to imagine just what those developments transpired to be. I, of course, did not at that time know that Bob McCloskey and later Amy Crosby in Sacramento had been or were in any way already involved, and what facts or evidence they might have been aware of prior to me handing over my copy documents to Michaela Clinch. I did not have long to wait though and, when they were revealed to me, I was truly astonished!

Chapter Seven
Finally!

On Thursday 1st December 2016, David J Sesma, an FBI Special Agent drove with a colleague to an old people's home in California. On stating that he wished to see Silas Duane Boston he was at once told, "He has gone to Paradise!" Taking into account the fact that Sesma knew Boston was an elderly man, he obviously took that to mean that Boston had died. After everything, that could only have resulted in instant enormous and profound dismay. However, after an explanation about what was really meant by Boston going to Paradise, Agent Sesma and his colleague went back to their vehicle. They then drove to the Seaview Rehabilitation and Wellness Centre in the town of Paradise, in California. They there, to the absolute astonishment of all the staff, arrested one of the home's residents, namely 75-year-old Silas Duane Boston for the murders of Christopher Farmer and Peta Frampton in 1978. Boston was then taken to Sacramento.

I recall thinking, when I heard that part of the story, that if Boston had indeed died, Paradise would have perhaps been the very last location where he might have been expected to then spend eternity. An obviously deeply shocked Boston, on arrival in Sacramento, was booked in and finally locked up in the jail there. I just wish I could somehow have been there to witness it all! Without a doubt, his arrest was so very many years later than it should have been. The following day I was telephoned by an obviously equally elated Michaela Clinch and told of Boston's arrest. As I was letting that enormous news sink in, she immediately went on to ask me if I would be prepared to fly to California. That was in order for me to give evidence concerning my part in the original investigation. My evidence was to include the requirement to swear and certify that certain of my retained copied documents to be used at Boston's trial were absolutely true copies I had made of the lost originals that had at one time been in my possession. Perhaps unsurprisingly, I immediately replied that I most certainly would be willing to go to the US I was absolutely overjoyed and could hardly believe what had finally transpired after so very many years.

FBI Agent Sesma, was a very experienced Criminal Investigator and, like Detective Clinch, had previously dealt with various *cold* criminal cases. Boston's long overdue arrest followed very close cooperation, hard work and enormous dedication in the US involving a number of people. These included Detectives Amy Crosby, Janine LeRose, Special Agent David Sesma with an unnamed FBI colleague, and an excellent team of no less than four very experienced Sacramento US Attorneys, namely Phillip A Talbert, United States Attorney for the Eastern District of California, Matthew D Segal, Jeremy J Kelly and Heiko P Coppola, all Assistant US Attorneys based in Sacramento.

Everything that led up to the final arrest of Boston had, of course, led on from Christopher Farmer's sister Penny, and her mother Audrey Farmer, who had been moved to ask for the murder case to be re-opened. That, assisted by an almost forgotten deteriorating file of old documents re-discovered at the bottom of a cardboard box in a garden shed of all places. Those documents ought never to have existed at all in the normal way of things. Without that old bundle of papers, a great deal of critical information would never have been available. That is why I said earlier that if anyone other than myself had originally been involved, they would likely never have routinely copied all the original documents, and/or actually kept possession of those copies for all the years that followed. There would have been little, other than my own memory of many of the key facts of the case and that would not have been enough at all.

There was a requirement that a particular process was necessary in the US legal system before criminal proceedings against Boston could commence. I was told that he was arrested by the FBI and not Detective Crosby and Janine le Rose because the case was a Federal one. In a similar case in England, he would simply have been arrested by the Police. A Criminal Complaint document was prepared in Sacramento that took the form of a twenty-eight-page very detailed Affidavit produced and signed by FBI Agent David Sesma. That Affidavit was sworn before Kendall J Newman, a US Magistrate Judge, on 1st December 2016 at the United States District Court for the Eastern District of California. The Affidavit, in disclosing what the SPD and the FBI already knew, also contained a great deal of information that was extracted from my old copied documents file. The affidavit resulted in an arrest warrant being issued after the Magistrate Judge had considered all the information within that lengthy document, a good deal of which made for quite harrowing reading. I found that the affidavit, perhaps surprisingly, was actually published in full on the internet just after Boston's arrest It proved, in parts, to be an enormous and unexpected revelation to me.

Just prior to Boston's arrest, as I have mentioned previously, I had not been told of the nature of the 'considerable progress' made during the US fresh investigation, Detective Clinch having been asked not to disclose what that progress was. I, of course, always knew the reason, that being because it was feared that if Boston somehow heard of his impending arrest, albeit he would hardly have heard it from me, directly or indirectly, he would abscond if at all possible, that being something he had apparently done in the past on quite a number of occasions.

Because of its overall sensational contents, what now follows is a typed copy of the entire twenty-eight-page Affidavit signed by Agent Sesma. As I read it on my computer screen for the first time, the whole horrific story was finally revealed to me. The Affidavit, with the US spelling, of some words unaltered, is preceded by a copy of the original 1st December 2016 Complaint document. It is followed by a copy of the original four-page Grand Jury Indictment of Boston that followed on 8th of December 2016. The reproduced documents might serve to give some small insight as to how the US criminal legal system worked on this case. I have inserted a few of my own comments at intervals within the relevant Affidavit pages:

AO 91 (Rev. 11/11) Criminal Complaint

UNITED STATES DISTRICT COURT

for the

Eastern District of California

FILED

DEC - 1 2016

CLERK, U.S. DISTRICT COURT
EASTERN DISTRICT OF CALIFORNIA
BY _____
DEPUTY CLERK

United States of America	)
v.	)
	) Case No.
	)
	) **2**16 - MJ - 2 0 6 KJN
SILAS DUANE BOSTON	)
Defendant(s)	)

CRIMINAL COMPLAINT

I, the complainant in this case, state that the following is true to the best of my knowledge and belief.

Between on or about the date(s) of   June 29, 1978, and July 6, 1978, within the special maritime and territorial jurisdiction of the United States, the defendant(s) violated:

Code Section	*Offense Description*
18 U.S.C. § § 7 & 1111(a) Maritime Murder	

This criminal complaint is based on these facts:

(see attachment)

☒ Continued on the attached sheet.

_____
Complainant's signature

FBI Special Agent David J. Sesma
Printed name and title

Sworn to before me and signed in my presence.

Date: **Dec 1, 2016**

_____
Judge's signature

City and state: **Sacramento, CA**

Kendall J. Newman, U.S. Magistrate Judge
Printed name and title

91

AFFIDAVIT IN SUPPORT OF AN APPLICATION
FOR A COMPLAINT AND ARREST WARRANT

I, David J Sesma, being first duly sworn, hereby depose and state as follows:

INTRODUCTION AND AGENT QUALIFICATIONS

1. I am employed by the Federal Bureau of Investigation (FBI) as a Special Agent.

As a Special Agent of the FBI, I am authorized to investigate violations of laws of the United States, and I am a law enforcement officer with authority to execute arrest and search warrants under the authority of the United States. I have been employed by the FBI since July 2004 and am currently assigned to the Sacramento Field Office, where I am investigating complex financial crimes. Prior to this assignment, I was assigned to the Fairfield Resident Agency of the FBI, where I investigated violent crimes. Included in my duties in the enforcement of all laws related to violent crime including, but not limited to, murder and crimes committed in the special maritime and territorial jurisdiction of the United States. I have received Specialized training in evidence collection and behavioral analysis and developed experience in various criminal investigations. I have also received training pertaining to the investigation of cold cases and I am a member of the Sacramento Field Office Behavioral Analysis Team which consults and investigates cold case homicides and other violent crimes.

OFFENSE

2. The FBI and the City of Sacramento Police Department (SPD) Cold Case Unit are investigating SILAS DUANE

BOSTON (BOSTON) for the 1978 premeditated maritime murders of CHRISTOPHER FARMER (FARMER) and PETA FRAMPTON (FRAMPTON).

The federal murder statutes in effect in 1978 provided:

Murder is the unlawful killing of a human being with malice aforethought. Every murder perpetrated by poison, lying in wait, or any other kind of wilful, deliberate, malicious, and premeditated killing; or committed in the perpetration of, or attempt to perpetrate, any arson, rape, burglary or robbery; or perpetrated from a premeditated design, unlawfully and maliciously to effect the death of any human being other than him who is killed, is murder in the first degree.

Any other murder is murder in the second degree.

18 U.S.C. 1111(a) (1948). The special maritime and territorial jurisdiction at the time included:

The high seas, any other waters within the admiralty and maritime jurisdiction of the United States and out of the jurisdiction of any particular state, and any vessel belonging in whole or in part to the United States or any citizen thereof, or to any corporation created by or under the laws of the United States, or of any State, Territory, District, or possession thereof, when such a vessel is within the admiralty and maritime jurisdiction of the United States and out of the jurisdiction of any particular State.

18 U.S.C. § 7(1) (1952).

3. BOSTON committed the murders by drowning FARMER and FRAMPTON in the Caribbean Sea off Guatemala. BOSTON bound his victims and caused them to go off *The Justin B*, a boat that BOSTON, a United States citizen, owned. The United States Attorney's Office informs

me that there is federal jurisdiction over these extraterritorial crimes because BOSTON, who is a United States citizen, committed the murders while on a boat that he owned. Maritime murder is a crime against the United States. *See* 18 U.S.C. §§ 1111,7(1). District courts have jurisdiction over such offences. *See* 18 U.S.C. § 3231. Venue is proper in whatever district the defendant is arrested or first brought on the maritime charge. *See 18* U.S.C. § 3238. Because the federal murder statute provides for the death penalty, there is no applicable statute of limitations. *See* 18 U.S.C. § 3281.

4. I have not included every fact that is known to me from my investigation, but rather only those facts that I believe are necessary to establish probable cause for this complaint and the issuance of an arrest warrant.

INVESTIGATION

5. On May 9, 2016, I met with SPD Detective Amy Crosby, who explained to me that she had been conducting an investigation into the 1968 disappearance of MARY LOU BOSTON (MARY LOU), BOSTON's former wife. Also during the meeting, I was introduced to Detective Michaela Clinch of the Greater Manchester Police Department (GMP) in the United Kingdom who was participating via teleconference. The SPD received a missing person's report for MARY LOU on September 26, 1968. The SPD investigated the case and were unable to locate MARY LOU. BOSTON convinced the investigating officer in 1968 that MARY LOU had taken funds from their joint bank account and run off with another man. But MARY LOU never reappeared to her family and shows up in no records indicating her survival after her disappearance. Detective

Crosby explained to me that during her investigation of MARY LOU's disappearance, she became aware of the murder of FARMER and FRAMPTON off the coast of Guatemala in 1978. Detective Crosby learned of the murders, contacted the GMP, and received records from GMP Detective Clinch.

(Author's Note: I had thought Crosby, without any old documents, could only have known of the Guatemala murders after contact from the GMP during 2015/16, but there was another unexpected reason.)

I have obtained copies of and reviewed numerous reports from the GMP, SPD, INTERPOL (International Police), and other government agencies in my investigation. I have also reviewed other supporting documentation including autopsy reports, port records, emails, letters, family photographs, and documents compiled by the victim's family.

Original Investigation of FARMER and FRAMPTON Disappearances

6. Much of my knowledge of FARMER and FRAMPTON comes from records that I received from GMP. The GMP records compilation is made chiefly of a working file that Detective Clinch collected from the retired GMP detective who investigated the FARMER/FRAMPTON disappearance in the late 1970s and early 1980s. The records were preserved because the retired GMP detective maintained copies in the garden shed of his home in England.

7. I learned from the GMPs records that FARMER and FRAMPTON, former residents of Cheshire, England, decided

to travel abroad for approximately one year, beginning in December 1977. FARMER and FRAMPTON were dating at the time they left the United Kingdom and were both approximately 25 years old. FARMER had recently graduated from medical school and FRAMPTON had recently graduated from university with a degree in law. The couple first travelled to Australia, where FARMER worked as a medical doctor for a few months at the After Hours Medical Centre in Brisbane, Australia. From there, the couple travelled to the Americas.

8. Throughout their travels, FARMER and FRAMPTON remained in frequent contact with their families through postcards, letters and by telephone. In a letter dated May 19, 1978, FRAMPTON wrote to her mother that she and FARMER were touring around Guadalajara, Mexico. In the same letter, I noted a date of May 24, 1978, and FRAMPTON indicated that she and FARMER had made their way to Oaxaca, Mexico. In a letter dated June 6, 1978, FRAMPTON wrote from "The Marin Hotel" in Belize. FRAMPTON wrote that she and FARMER had travelled through Belize City, Belize and then to Cay Caulker, Belize. FRAMPTON said she intended to subsequently travel to New Orleans, Louisiana, to visit a friend. Later in the same letter, FRAMPTON wrote the date June 13, 1978, and stated, "Sorry, I forgot to post this in Belize on Sat so am adding a little now as all our plans have changed we originally meant to get the bus to Merida but knew an American called Dwayne (sic) who owns a Belizean boat called the '*Justin B*' offered to take us up to Chetumal (Mexico) by sail so we decided to do that." FRAMPTON then writes, "...Dwayne (sic) wanted to take the boat down to Costa Rica to sell it, anyway, we thought it was an opportunity

not to be missed espcly (sic) as Chris wanted sailing experience."

9. The final letter written by FRAMPTON was received by the FRAMPTON family in Manchester, England in or around early August 1978. The envelope was postmarked, "Livingston, 18th July 1978." (Livingston is a town in Guatemala.) The sender's name and address listed on the letter was, P A Frampton, *The Justin B.*" FRAMPTON begins the letter by writing "On the way to Hunting Cay" and dates the letter June 28, 1978. FRAMPTON continues to write, "Dear Mum, we have just set off from Placentia (sic), a small fishing port in the south of Belize and it's about 7 am." In the same letter FRAMPTON added the date of June 29, 1978, and wrote, "Well, we had a perfect sail and reached Hunting Cay at abt (sic) 11 am."

FRAMPTON later wrote,

"Another reason I wouldn't mind ending my sailing career now – I'm down as a sailor on the papers! – as is the 2 sons of Duane. They are 12 and 13 years but behave more like 8 and 9 and I find I have no patience at all with them. Of course, they squabble most of the time and I now see how irritating we must have been in that respect. But on a boat there's nowhere you can go. What makes it worse is that Duane curses and puts them down continually, often when things are not going quite right like when we didn't get one of the anchors up because the motor wasn't working to give us leverage and we subsequently went back for it and managed to retrieve it abt $100 worth."

FRAMPTON ends her final letter by writing, "Enough of the future. I don't think there's any more news—nothing much happens on a boat. Lots of love Pete." The

FRAMPTON family never received another letter from FRAMPTON. Neither the FRAMPTON family nor the FARMER family ever heard from the couple again.

10. I learned from the GMP in or about September 1978, the families of FARMER and FRAMPTON became concerned because they had not heard from the couple since FRAMPTON's last letter, which was postmarked on or about July 18, 1978. As a result, FARMER's father, Charles Beupre Bell Farmer, began making his own enquiries in order to locate FARMER and FRAMPTON. His efforts included corresponding with the British Foreign and Commonwealth Office as well as individuals in Belize, Guatemala and the United States. Charles Farmer shared this correspondence with the GMP. I have reviewed the correspondence and accompanying documentation.

11. I reviewed a letter to the FARMER family, dated September 29, 1978, written by Belizean Acting Harbour Master A F Mahler which confirmed that FRAMPTON and FARMER were on board *The Justin B*. Mahler wrote that he reviewed and obtained photocopies of Belizean port records. Mahler states that in September of 1978:

"The latest information I have regarding the "*Justin B*" is that she sailed from the port of Dangriga in Belize bound for Puerto Cortes Honduras on the 26th of June 1978. The captain of the boat was an American named Duane Boston. As you can see from the attached photocopies of the ship's clearance from Dangriga on 26th June, your son and Miss Frampton were members of the crew for this voyage. On the 9th August 1978, the "*Justin B*" again entered the port of Dangriga, Belize. Apparently, it had returned to Livingston (sic) directly from Puerto Cortes and then came on to Dangriga from there.

Your son and Miss Frampton were not part of the crew for this voyage."

I reviewed the three-page document attached to the letter from A F Mahler. The first page lists the port of registry as "Belize" and the "Name of the Master" as "Duane Boston." On the bottom of the page is the apparent signature of DUANE BOSTON. The second page is titled "Port of Belize-Entry Outwards" and the ship's name is listed as "*Justin B.*" The port of Destination is listed as "Puerto Cortes, Honduras." The third page of the report is a "Crew List" which listed the following crew and passengers and their occupations:

Name Age Nationality Occupations:

Duane Boston 37 American Master

Chris Farmer 25 British Sailor

Peter Frampton 24 British Sailor

Vince Boston 13 American Sailor

Russell Boston 12 American Sailor

Later, on the same page, I saw a signature of the "Captain" which appeared to be signed by DUANE BOSTON. The stamp on the form lists the date as June 26, 1978, "Custom-House-Dangriga-Belize."

12. The FARMER family received a letter from the British Consulate in Guatemala dated October 23, 1978, which indicated that when *The Justin B*. arrived in Guatemala, FRAMPTON and FARMER were no longer aboard. The letter states, "The Foreign Office will probably have told you that we contacted the Immigration office in Livingston. Their records show that *The Justin B* entered Livingston on 6 July 1978 with only three passengers aboard: SILAS DUANE BOSTON and his two young sons. The Immigration authorities in Livingston also told us that Silas Duane Boston

is resident in California. You probably know that, as a result, the Foreign Office has asked the British Consulate General in San Francisco to try and contact Mr Boston and enquire where your son disembarked and whether he knew of his future travel plans.

13. The FARMER family received a report dated July 8, 1978, written in Spanish, that detailed the recovery by volunteer firefighters (otherwise known as "Bomberos" in Spanish) of two corpses floating in the ocean off Punta de Manabique, Guatemala. I have reviewed an English translation of the report which states the following:

"At the request of the Justice of the Peace of this port, we were transported by a unit of the Marines to Punta de Manabique. On arrival at the place mentioned we became aware that approximately 200 metres from the beach two corpses were floating in the sea. We had to go into the water since we had already attempted to lift them from the deck of a small boat supplied by local commissioners. When we were in the water we became aware that one of them, the male, was wearing blue canvas jacket, and blue shorts, the body was decomposed and we could not obtain major details of complexion, hair, face etc. This corpse had its hands bound behind the back and legs and ankles were also bound; around the neck, it had a yellow nylon string 15 metres long tied to a 'shock block' (part of the engine of an automobile), it had a bullet hole in the right leg and signs of torture. The other corpse, the female, was wearing a green T-shirt, no brassier, green shorts, and was also decomposed; her hands were bound in the back as were her legs and ankles, and from the string to the bottom of the sea hung part of the engine of an automobile commonly called "Espejo con toda y su corona" She had a plastic bag covering her head, as a hood, tied around her neck, and it was observed that her hair was blonde, her age was between 15 and 18 years, 1.65 metres high. After picking up the bodies they were taken from Punta de Manabique to the dock of the Marines at Santo Tomas and from there to the Puerto Barrios National Amphitheatre in Unit 78 of this Company."

14. I know from reviewing maps of the area that Punta de Manabique, where the bodies were recovered, is a peninsular about 10 miles Northeast of Livingston. Below is a screen capture of a Google Maps image of Livingston, Punta de Manabique, and parts of the coast of Belize and Honduras.

(Author's Note: That screen capture referred to is not included here as it was far too indistinct to copy adequately from the Affidavit. My own included prepared map is of the same area).

Note by D Sesma: Throughout my investigation, I have seen "Peter" used interchangeably with "Peta." I believe that individuals may have mistaken FRAMPTON's first name for "Peter" given the similar pronunciation between "Peta" and "Peter" as well as the name of the singer Peter Frampton at the time. I believe that the notations "Peter Frampton" here and elsewhere are in fact references to PETA FRAMPTON.

15. The FARMER family also obtained a letter written by Dr. Angel Maria Vasquez Cuellar of the "Department of Forensic Medicine, Judicial Power, Department of Guatemala" dated February 7, 1979.

The letter documented Dr. Cuellar's July 10, 1978 autopsy of the recovered bodies as follows:

101

"With reference to your note of 6 February 1979, I hereby inform you that on 9 July 1978 two unidentified corpses were brought to the Amphitheatre of the national hospital of this city: one was male and the other female, and they were sent to us by the local provisional Justice of the Peace, to perform an autopsy. These corpses were found floating near the village of Punta de Manabiqe on 8 July 1978 at 15.30 hours.

In the protocol of Autopsy no. 3853, on 10 July at 9.30 hours, is recorded the unidentified female corpse, a young adult whose age is not calculated due to the advanced stage of decomposition, wearing no dress and covered only with a white nylon panty; her height was approximately 1.65 metres and weight approximately 50-55 kilos; she had fish bites over her body and the aspect of the corpse is monstrous. The examination of the viscera shows congestion of the lungs, and upon the cutting dripped fetid foamy blood serum. The efficient cause of death was recorded as asphyxia by submersion."

In the protocol of Autopsy no. 3854 of 10 July 1978 at 10:30 hours is recorded the unidentified male corpse of approximately 65 kilos of weight and 1.67 metres tall; a young adult whose age cannot be calculated by the advanced stage of decomposition; his aspect is monstrous and has fish bites over his body. From the examination of the viscera is reported lung congestion with intra-lung material. The efficient cause of death was recorded as asphyxia by submersion."

16. The FARMER family received a letter from the Foreign and Commonwealth Office dated June 29, 1979, which indicated the recovered bodies were identified as FARMER and FRAMPTON:

"An examination of five bodies was carried out at the cemetery on 10 April. This number of exhumations was necessary because the stakes which had earlier marked the plots of unidentified bodies buried in the cemetery had, in the course of time, been removed. During the exhumations, the bodies of your son and Miss Frampton were positively identified. They were reburied immediately in plots 58 and 59. The Consul telegraphed this information to us on 10 April and, you being then in Portugal, our Consul in Lisbon conveyed the news to you on the following day. We informed Mrs Frampton."

17. Included in the documents that the GMP provided to the US investigators was a report dated April 16, 1979, prepared by Dr Gustavo Berger R of the "Oral Medicine and Surgery Guatemala, CA" Dr. Berger wrote that he examined two corpses which were exhumed from the cemetery at Puerto Barrios. Dr. Berger described his examination and comparison of the dental records of FARMER and FRAMPTON supplied from England with the dental structures of the corpses exhumed from the cemetery at Puerto Barrios. He found that the dental records matched the corpses, and concluded the bodies were those of FARMER and FRAMPTON. The GMP also provided a report written by James Kenneth Holt, a Doctor of Dental Surgery in Manchester who reviewed the background information on the case, the report by Dr. Berger from Guatemala, and the dental records of FRAMPTON and FARMER. Holt confirmed Dr. Berger's findings and the identification of the bodies of FARMER and FRAMPTON.

18. I learned from the GMP that several attempts were made to contact BOSTON for information about what

happened to FARMER and FRAMPTON. For example, the FARMER family received a letter dated November 29, 1978, from the Foreign and Commonwealth Office, stating:

"Our Consulate General in San Francisco spoke to Mr Duane Boston by telephone on 30 October. The address through which they contacted him, which we assume remains the same, is as given in my letter to you of 17 October: Box 134 Smith's Flat, California 95222. Duane Boston said that he remembered Chris and Peter very well and that they had been frequent passengers on his boat. He said that he agreed to take them from Belize to Puerto Cortes. Stops were made at various islands but as *The Justin B.* subsequently required repairs the two passengers disembarked at a peninsular across the bay from Livingston. It appears that their intention was to hire a native boat. Boston said that he thought he saw them in Livingston boarding a ferry during the second week in July but cannot be sure. He did not know their ultimate destination but said they could be heading for San Andreas Island or Trinidad or they might go to Colombia or Peru."

(Author's note: Those indications by Boston, but for Peta's letter, would have caused enquiries to trace them to be made in entirely the wrong areas).

19. One of the documents provided by the GMP was entitled "Greater Manchester Police Statement of Witness" and dated August 22, 1979. Charles Farmer provided the statement to the GMP in which he attests that he attempted to contact BOSTON by telephone but instead spoke with BOSTON's father Russell Boston. Farmer then received a return telephone call from BOSTON on or about January 25,

1979. Farmer told the GMP, that to the best of his recollection, the following conversation took place with BOSTON via the telephone:

Author's note: This conversation has already been reproduced earlier in this book.

Q. "Is that Duane Boston?"

A. "Yes".

Q. "The Mr. Duane Boston, owner of *The Justin B*?"

A. "Yes, I was."

Q. "This is Charles Farmer, father of Dr. Christopher Farmer who was on board your boat with Miss Frampton last year. I would like to ask you a few questions, as we have not heard from them since Hunting Cay, in June."

A. "Yes, I remember them. I spoke to someone from the British Consul and told them all about them."

Q. "Yes, quite, you landed them where?"

A. "Near Porto Barrios."

Q. "In Guatemala?"

A. "Yes, in Guatemala."

Q. "What sort of coast?"

A. "The beach."

Q. "How were they dressed?"

A. "I can't remember—jeans or something."

Q. "Had Chris got his medical bag?"

A. "His what?"

Q. "Well Chris was a medical doctor, and he was going to another medical appointment, he would have his medical bag."

A. "No. A duffle bag."

Q. "Were they alright for money?"

A. "They seemed to be alright."

Q. "Had they got their air tickets to USA?"

A. "I wouldn't know."

Q. "Any idea where they might have stayed if not in hotels in Livingston?"

A. "I expect they caught a ferry."

Q. "Do you know who might have posted the letter on 18th July?"

A. "No."

Q. "Any mention of Chris going to Trinidad and Peta going to New Orleans?"

A. "Might have been mentioned in discussion. They intended to sail to Costa Rica, but they were in no hurry."

Q. "We understand you had some trouble with the boat, it was damaged?"

A. "Yes, the mast was split.

Q. "Was it gale damage?"

A. "Yes."

Q. "Where was this?"

A. "Off Porto Barrios."

Q. "You were at Hunting Cay on 29th June, when did you drop them off, what date and when did you get to Livingston?"

A. "I dropped them off somewhere about the 3rd to the 6th July. I don't remember."

Q. "We have records showing you entered Livingston on the 6th."

A. "Don't remember but if you say so."

Q. "Where were you seen by fishermen?"

A. "I don't remember any fishermen."

Q. "Were there any drugs aboard the boat?"

A. "No."

Q. "Were they clear on their next destination?"

A. "They were travelling to Mexico, then changed to go to Costa Rica."

Q. "Do you still have the boat's log or any details of the trip?"

A. "No."

Q. "How would you expect them to get to Livingston?"

A. "Hire a Dhorry."

Q. "If they had gone through normal channels in Livingston, what problems would they have arriving in Honduras?"

A. "Everybody does it."

Q. "How would they get into Guatemala if no entry stamps on their passports?"

A. "No questions are asked."

Q. "Are there any Communist guerillas in Guatemala?"

A. "I've not heard of any, but natives think there are."

Q. "Had they mentioned going to Peru or Colombia?"

A. "Just talk, and mention of San Andreas."

Q. "Did they pay for their time onboard?"

A. "Yes, 500 dollars." (I have enquired amongst friends and this is regarded as a ridiculously large figure, perhaps $50 each is more realistic. In fact, I calculate Peta and Chris could have had anything between £500 to £1000 in currency in their joint possession at this time).

Q. "What cargo did you pick up at Dangriga?"

A. "Did not have any cargo – only coconuts and mangoes for ballast."

Q. Have you any idea what might have happened to them?"

A. "No."

Q. There is no trace of them ever having been in Livingston, except your report of seeing them on a ferry."

A. "Oh—I guess I saw them around the 9th boarding a ferry but when I had walked round they had gone. Let me know if you hear anything about them."

20. I learned from my conversation with the GMP that the matter was referred by GMP to Interpol and US law enforcement. In a letter to Charles Farmer dated July 29, 1981, Sergeant (sic) James R Kelly of the San Rafael Police Department wrote of his investigation of BOSTON in 1981 for the abduction of his son Justin, for whom *The Justin B*, was named.

(Note by D Sesma: This (abduction) case was ultimately dismissed. I am not relying upon it for probable cause.)

Kelly observed that "During my investigation of Boston, he managed to elude law enforcement throughout Northern California; this was an extremely intensive search as Boston had possession of the child and it was feared he would leave the country." Responding to a request from Interpol, Kelly asked BOSTON about the disappearance of CHRIS and PETA:

"At the time I interviewed Boston, I had thoroughly reviewed the information from Inspector Sacks (of the GMP). As I have related earlier, Boston became visibly upset when I informed him of the deaths of Dr. Farmer and Miss Frampton. Prior to this he had been very calm and was freely discussing the child abduction case with me. Boston was confused about exact dates except for the telephone call he made to his former wife, Kathe Quinn, from Livingston on July 16 or 17. He remembered this date because July 16 is his daughter's birthday and was the reason he made the call."

The Sacramento Police Department Cold Case Unit
Obtained Direct Evidence that
BOSTON Murdered FARMER and FRAMPTON

21. I learned from the GMP that the investigation of the deaths of FARMER and FRAMPTON eventually stalled and the case went cold. But I have also learned from SPD Detective Crosby that her recent investigation of the cold case disappearance of MARY LOU BOSTON yielded important new evidence about the deaths of Farmer and FRAMPTON. In my review of SPD reports from the investigation into the disappearance of MARY LOU and my conversations with SPD Detective Crosby, I learned BOSTON's two sons, RUSSELL BOSTON (RB) and VINCE BOSTON (VB) provided detailed statements, photos, emails, and other evidence implicating BOSTON in the murder of FARMER and FRAMPTON. RB and VB both say that they saw their father murder FARMER and FRAMPTON. At the time of the murders, RB was 11 years old and VB was 13 years old.

22. On October 13, 2015, VB spoke with Detective Crosby via the telephone and the conversation was recorded. VB stated the trip to Belize occurred after an incident in Sacramento, California. RB and VB shared a room next door to BOSTON and they heard a female yelling at BOSTON in the middle of the night telling BOSTON to stop. Soon after the incident with the female, BOSTON took RB and VB to get passports and buy snorkelling gear at Big 5 Sporting Goods. BOSTON then drove his sons in a truck through Mexico until they reached Belize. BOSTON bought a boat in Belize and named it *The Justin B* after his other son Justin. BOSTON and his sons VB and RB then sailed around the

Cays and took tourists out on the boat. BOSTON charged tourists money for 110ravelled110g or scuba diving. BOSTON was not licensed to provide guided tours or meals while in Belize.

23. VB told Detective Crosby that while in Belize City, BOSTON and his sons picked up a young couple named Chris Farmer and Peter Frampton who were tourists from England. VB recalled that they would constantly write letters home detailing their trip. VB recalled FARMER had a field camera and he believed BOSTON kept it. VB indicated he had one of the photos which depicts FARMER, VB and RB standing on *The Justin B.*

24. VB told Detective Crosby that BOSTON would become very violent when he drank alcohol and sometimes he would cuss and yell at RB. On one such occasion, FARMER told BOSTON to leave RB alone. BOSTON tried to hit FARMER, missed, and fell into the water. FARMER and FRAMPTON laughed at BOSTON after he fell into the water. Soon after the incident with FARMER, according to VB and RB, BOSTON began plotting FARMER's and FRAMPTON's death.

25. VB described the murders to Detective Crosby. At the time, *The Justin B* was far out from the port and anchored in the harbour near the port of Livingston, Guatemala.

(*Author's note: This was at least VB's recent recollection of where the boat was at that time*).

One night at dusk, BOSTON told FARMER to pull up the anchor. As FARMER pulled up the anchor BOSTON struck FARMER repeatedly in the head with a wooden "billy club".

The "billy club" eventually broke and FARMER screamed, "what's your game? What's your game?" while BOSTON assaulted him. When FRAMPTON exited the galley of *The Justin B*, BOSTON threatened to shoot her with a spear gun. BOSTON attempted to stab FARMER in the chest with a fillet knife but the knife broke. BOSTON then tackled FARMER and tied him up with ropes. BOSTON also bound FRAMPTON with ropes. BOSTON put FARMER in the front of the boat and put FRAMPTON down in the galley. BOSTON then forced VB to watch FRAMPTON for the night while she was tied up with ropes.

26. The next morning BOSTON told FARMER and FRAMPTON he was going to take them somewhere isolated and tie them up to a tree so they could eventually escape but so BOSTON could also get away. BOSTON told FARMER and FRAMPTON that he just wanted their traveller's checks and wanted the couple to sign the checks over to him. BOSTON moved FRAMPTON to the rear of the boat and they were both "hogtied." BOSTON tied machine parts (used for ship ballast) to FARMER's and FRAMPTON's bindings. BOSTON put plastic bags over their heads and told FARMER and FRAMPTON he did not want them to see where they were. FRAMPTON and FARMER were still alive and could still breathe with the bags on their heads. *The Justin B* was a few miles out, in the deep water. BOSTON walked up and threw the machine parts overboard and then pushed FARMER overboard into the water. BOSTON then pushed FRAMPTON overboard and into the water. BOSTON looked at his watch and after three or four minutes stated, "OK, they are dead now."

(Author's note: Punta de Manabique, where the boat clearly must have been at that time, is some ten miles or so across the bay from Livingston. That distance from Livingston, when viewed from one side of the boat, could have caused Vincent Boston's recollection that the vessel, although close to the peninsular, as being a few miles out at sea).

27. VB related to Detective Crosby that FARMER had a medical bag with his name engraved on his tools, and BOSTON told RB and VB they needed to help him get rid of the evidence and remove FARMER's name from his tools. VB did not want to be part of getting rid of the evidence but BOSTON told him if they were caught they would all be killed. BOSTON took a hot piece of metal and melted FARMER's name off his tools. BOSTON had RB forge the traveller's checks so BOSTON could spend them.

28. On January 19, 2016, RB also provided a statement to Detective Crosby. RB told Detective Crosby that he, VB and BOSTON left Sacramento to go to Belize because of a "statutory rape" investigation involving BOSTON. RB explained to Detective Crosby that two days before FARMER and FRAMPTON were killed, BOSTON began yelling and punching RB on the boat. FARMER came to RB's defense and told BOSTON to leave RB alone. BOSTON did not stop punching RB so FARMER pushed BOSTON overboard and into the water. BOSTON was angry after the incident.

29. The next day, BOSTON told FARMER and FRAMPTON he was going to drop them off in Guatemala but it had to be at night because they did not have visas. Later in the day, at dusk, BOSTON told FARMER to pull the anchor up. As FARMER was pulling up the anchor BOSTON came

112

up behind FARMER with an "antique billy club" and hit FARMER on the back of the head. FARMER fell to his knees and BOSTON kept hitting him with the club. FARMER started screaming, "what's your game, what's your game" and was trying to cover his head. BOSTON took out a fillet knife and stabbed FARMER in the chest but the knife broke. FARMER told BOSTON, "I give up, I give up" and BOSTON stopped beating him. FARMER asked BOSTON why he had attacked him. BOSTON claimed it was because FARMER did not pay him for his services. FARMER told BOSTON he would be paid immediately. BOSTON told FARMER he was not going to drop him off in Livingston but rather off the peninsular where no one was around so he could get away before the police were called. BOSTON hurt his back during the attack and FARMER injected him with a muscle relaxer. BOSTON bound FARMER and FRAMPTON and then placed bags over their heads with holes cut in them so they could breathe.

30. RB told Detective Crosby that BOSTON steered *The Justin B* away from the shore and headed out to sea. FARMER and FRAMPTON were on the edge of the boat waiting to be dropped off onshore. BOSTON gathered machine parts used for ballast and set them next to FARMER and FRAMPTON. BOSTIN then tied the machine parts to FARMER and FRAMPTON with a rope. BOSTON stated, "ok we are right along the shore and it's really shallow so I'm going to push you guys right off, it's not very deep so you are going to just stand right up. Here we go." BOSTON pushed FARMER off first and dropped the weight in behind him. FRAMPTON started screaming, asking FARMER if he was OK. BOSTON pushed FRAMPTON off the boat and then pushed the weight

into the water. BOSTON filled the sails with air and *The Justin B* sailed away. No one said anything for a couple of hours then BOSTON stated, "You know I had to do that. They didn't give me a choice."

31. RB stated that BOSTON sailed *The Justin B* into Livingston, Guatemala. BOSTON took FARMER's and FRAMPTON's clothes and dropped them off at a local business. BOSTON steamed open and read the letters FRAMPTON had written. BOSTON re-sealed the letters and mailed them to FRAMPTON's family. BOSTON said it was better for the families to get the letters and think FARMER and FRAMPTON were still alive in Livingston, Guatemala. I believe BOSTON mailed this letter to FRAMPTON's family, as RB claims, because on July 8, 1978, ten days before the letter was postmarked, the bodies of FARMER and FRAMPTON were recovered from the sea by the "Bomberos".

(Authors note: The letter postmarked 18 July comprised 8 handwritten pages and it may be that the number of pages gave Russell Boston the impression that there was more than the one letter steamed open and read by Boston. That is unless there was a further letter or letters addressed to someone else).

32. RB stated that BOSTON took the boys to El Estor, Guatemala, for about a week after the murders. RB indicated that BOSTON was later told by INTERPOL that the bodies had washed up on shore, and they were tied to weights. BOSTON told RB that he told the investigators he had just dropped FARMER and FRAMPTON off and they were going

to get in a boat to head to another destination. RB sent Detective Crosby the following photograph in an email on January 27, 2016, which RB depicts FARMER on *The Justin B* with RB and VB.

33. I reviewed a report from Detective Crosby which documented her interview of Bryan Logsdon, a former friend of BOSTON. Logsdon spent one year with BOSTON travelling through Mexico in the early 1990s and last had contact with BOSTON in the year 2000. During their time together, BOSTON told Logsdon that he had committed a number of murders. Logsdon knows BOSTON because of Logsdon's prior friendship with RB, whom Logsdon described as "more of a brother than my real brother is."

34. BOSTON told Logsdon about a young couple he took out sailing while he was in Belize. BOSTON told him one of the victims was a doctor. BOSTON said he took the couple out and tied rocks or boat parts to them and put bags over their heads. BOSTON then threw the male into the water while he was still tied up to the weights. BOSTON said the female on the boat heard the splash of the male victim entering the water

115

and calling her boyfriend's name and after a couple of minutes, BOSTON threw the female into the water. BOSTON told Logsdon it was funny because when the bag burst over her head you could hear her screams through the bubbles that came up while she was drowning. BOSTON was telling the story and laughing because he had gotten away with it. BOSTON told Logsdon the story in a nonchalant manner as they were driving. BOSTON told Logsdon he learned from killing the two tourists that you should "gut someone when you are going to throw them in the water because otherwise, they are going to bloat and float ashore." BOSTON told Logsdon he killed the tourists for the fun of it and that Interpol tried to interview him about the murders but he would not travel back with them to Belize because he knew he would be arrested.

35. Logsdon stated if BOSTON knew he had talked to law enforcement he would fear for his family's safety and that BOSTON may still have contacts to get something done.

The FBI Investigation Obtained Corroborating Evidence

36. In my review of the police reports, letters and statements of RB and VB, in this case, I believe the murders of FRAMPTON and FARMER occurred between the dates of June 29, 1978 (the last letter written and dated by FRAMPTON) and July 6, 1978 (the date *The Justin B* returned to the Livingston port in Guatemala). The bodies of FRAMPTON and FARMER were recovered from the sea on July 8, 1978.

37. I received a copy of BOSTON's birth certificate from the California Department of Public Health, Center for Health Statistics. The birth certificate lists BOSTON's date of birth

as March 20, 1941, and birthplace as "Shasta Co. Hospital, Clear Creek, Rural Shasta." I know Shasta County is located in Northern California. I reviewed a report from the Marin County Sheriff's Department which was a booking sheet for an arrest of BOSTON on February 19, 1981. On the form, BOSTON's place of birth is listed as Redding, California. I reviewed a record from the US Department of Homeland Security which reflects BOSTON as holding a valid United States Passport as of June 1, 2015. Based upon these records I believe that at the time of the offence, BOSTON was a citizen of the United States of America.

38. On August 9, 2016, the FBI interviewed Alberto Mahler in Belize City. Mahler was the acting harbour director who sent a letter to Charles Farmer in 1978, as detailed in paragraph 11. Mahler recognised his signature on the letter. But he had no independent recollection of the circumstances. Mahler identified the photocopied documents attached to the letter as documents that would have been used by the Belize Port Authority at the time.

39. The FBI recently located and interviewed one of the Bomberos, Alicio Palacios, who recovered the bodies of FARMER and FRAMPTON, as described in paragraph 13. Palacios was shown the report labelled "Report of Miscellaneous Services" which detailed the recovery of the bodies from the sea. Palacios stated he recalled recovering the bodies and verified the report looked like the report in which they would document a report for service.

40. Dr. Cuellar, who performed the autopsy report detailed in paragraph 15, was recently located and interviewed by the FBI in Guatemala. Dr Cuellar is retired. Dr. Cuellar reviewed the letter dated February 7, 1979,

117

verified its authenticity, and recognised his signature at the bottom of the page.

41. I recently interviewed former Sergeant Kelly of the San Rafael Police Department. Kelly informed me he retired in 2004 but recalled interviewing BOSTON at the request of Interpol as detailed in paragraph 20. Kelly stated BOSTON told him he did have FRAMPTON and FARMER aboard his ship but dropped them off at their intended destination and watched them walk away.

(Author's note: Kelly's recollection to the FBI about Boston's account of the circumstances of his parting company with the couple will be seen to differ from what he actually wrote in his report.)

42. I interviewed RB on October 13, 2016, and he verified the statements he made to Detective Crosby. RB provided a briefcase to the FBI which contained old identification cards and a receipt for the original purchase of *The Justin B*. According to RB, *The Justin B* was originally named the "*Marcia P*" and it was purchased on April 19, 1978, by BOSTON and BOSTON's father, Russell Boston (who shares a first name with his grandson RB). RB verified his grandfather's signature and his father's signature on the receipt as the new owners of the boat.

43. RB told me he is still fearful of BOSTON because of his past experience with him and his violent 118ravelled. In the 1970s and 1980s, BOSTON fled from law enforcement numerous times after becoming aware of potential charges against him. RB told me BOSTON would flee to Mexico and was living there until his health started failing and he needed

medical care. RB told me BOSTON would again flee to Mexico if he knew of the current investigation. BOSTON speaks Spanish fluently. BOSTON is very vindictive and RB is unsure of who BOSTON has as contacts with in the "outlaw" world. RB told me that BOSTON does not telegraph his acts of violence; if he plans to retaliate, he plans his retaliation very carefully. BOSTON told RB in a conversation, "anything worse than a nigger is a nigger lover, anything worse than a nigger lover is a snitch."

44. RB states that he recalls BOSTON being intoxicated after the murders of FARMER and FRAMPTON and he threatened to kill the boys. BOSTON stated, "if there is a heaven they can find their mother." BOSTON told RB and VB how he killed their mother and about others he had killed. BOSTON stated he only regretted killing their mother and that the boys needed to die. While anchored offshore, BOSTON told RB that his pet parrot named SALTY did not need to die and that RB should take SALTY into town and give the bird away. BOSTON would not let VB accompany RB into town. AS RB left to take the parrot ashore, BOSTON told him that BOSTON would kill RB and VB quickly, but if RB did not return he would kill VB slowly and painfully. RB was not able to give SALTY away and ended up rowing back to his father and VB with the parrot. RB had tears in his eyes as he was rowing back to the boat because he thought he was going to die. Upon arriving back at *The Justin B*, RB realized that while RB had been gone, BOSTON had sold *The Justin B* to a passing American couple who had been interested in the boat. BOSTON told RB and VB to pack their bags because they were going back to the United States.

45. I interviewed VB on October 13, 2016, and he verified the previous statements he made to Detective Crosby. VB also added he is afraid of BOSTON and stated BOSTON is capable of sending someone after him despite his health problems. VB will feel safer once BOSTON is in the custody of law enforcement. I reviewed the statement VB provided to Detective Crosby on October 13, 2015. VB stated that BOSTON lived in Mexico in the 1980s and Southern California in the 1990s. BOSTON usually travelled into Mexico when things were "hot". BOSTON equates "hot" as being wanted by law enforcement. If BOSTON wanted to travel into Mexico, he would usually drive across the border.

46. RB and VB are estranged from one another and their father.

BOSTON's Statements about Other Murders

47. BOSTON has told various people over the years since MARY LOU's disappearance that he killed her. Logsdon provided a statement to Detective Crosby in which he said BOSTON told Logsdon about the murder of MARY LOU. BOSTON said that MARY LOU was going to leave BOSTON in a divorce so he took her to one of his favourite shooting places and when she got out of the truck BOSTON said to her "run bitch" and she started running. BOSTON fired shots at her with his gun and hit her. BOSTON told Logsdon that he was unsure if he had hit her on the back of her skull or on the base of her skull but the shot did not kill her. BOSTON stated he walked up to her and she looked up at him and said, "but what about the kids?" BOSTON told Logsdon that after she asked him the question BOSTON just "snuffed the bitch."

BOSTON said he "snuffed" her in a creek bed and it caved in on her and that she will not be found for a "million years."

48. RB provided a statement to Detective Crosby about MARY LOU on January 19, 2016. BOSTON provided the details about his murder of MARY LOU directly to RB. RB stated BOSTON got MARY LOU to get into his car on the day he killed her by saying he just wanted to talk to her. Once she got in the car, BOSTON told her he was going to kill her and she begged him not to kill her. BOSTON told MARY LOU to run from the car and eventually she did. When she ran, BOSTON shot her. BOSTON then went up to her after she was shot and bleeding and crying and her last words were "what about the kids, what about the kids?" and then she died. BOSTON buried her and had blisters on his hands afterwards.

49. VB also provided a statement to Detective Crosby on October 13, 2015, related to the murder of MARY LOU. VB stated BOSTON told him directly he killed MARY LOU and buried her in a place that no one would ever find her. BOSTON told VB he shot her as she was running away and the last thing she said was "Duane, what about the kids?" and then he shot her in the back and buried her. VB heard from BOSTON's mother (VB's grandmother) and BOSTON himself, that MARY LOU was the only victim BOSTON regretted killing and that he killed her for his kids.

50. BOSTON also told Logsdon about another couple who had hired BOSTON while he was in Belize. BOSTON took them to a small island in a small rubber raft, robbed them, cut their throats and left them in the jungle. Soon after killing this couple, BOSTON sold his boat to an unknown American couple. Logsdon did not know if RB or VB had witnessed this other couple being murdered.

51. During my interview with RB on October 13, 2016, RB mentioned a German couple who had wanted to travel to Roatan, Honduras, after the murders of FRAMPTON and FARMER. *The Justin B* 122ravelled from Livingston, Guatemala to San Pedro when a huge storm arrived. The Germans became scared and began to paddle on both sides of *The Justin B* towards the shore. BOSTON joked that they looked like "Vikings" with the way they paddled. The Germans did not have visas to enter San Pedro so BOSTON helped them ashore in a smaller boat carried onboard *The Justin B*. RB gave me a scrap of paper from among the documents that BOSTON had given RB. It had a German address on it. Law enforcement in Germany located a German citizen who stated he had 122ravelled in Central America in 1978. The FBI has not been able to link BOSTON to the murder of any Europeans besides FARMER and FRAMPTON.

52. BOSTON also told Logsdon about a time a female told BOSTON she had been sexually assaulted by five drug dealers out of Sacramento. BOSTON said he helped her plan how to get back at the guys who had assaulted her. BOSTON told Logsdon he pulled up, jumped out of the car, and fired his handgun at the group of guys, hitting three of them. BOSTON told Logsdon he had to destroy the gun after the shooting. The investigation to this point has not been able to corroborate BOSTON's claims about this shooting.

53. The investigation has, however, corroborated another claim BOSTON has made about killing someone. During an interview with Detective Crosby, RB advised that he had been told by BOSTON that BOSTON had been involved in a hit and run traffic accident on Lemon Hill Avenue, Sacramento,

California in the late 1960s or early 1970s. BOSTON told RB that the victim had been killed and that the incident had been in the local newspaper. Detective Crosby was able to locate a Sacramento Bee article describing the June 10, 1972 hit and run traffic death of Marshall Williams on Lemon Hill Avenue near Stockton Boulevard in Sacramento.

54. Today, I arrested BOSTON in Paradise, which is in the Eastern District of California.

CONCLUSION

I submit that this affidavit establishes probable cause that SILAS DUANE BOSTON has committed two violations of 18 U.S.C. §§ 7 and 1111(a) – maritime murder. I request an arrest warrant for SILAS DUANE BOSTON be issued. I swear under penalty of perjury that the foregoing is true and correct to the best of my knowledge, information and belief.

(Author's note: Para 54 above states BOSTON had already been arrested by Agent Sesma so the issue and execution of the requested arrest warrant presumably was to ensure the continued detention of BOSTON pending a Grand Jury Hearing).

Respectfully submitted: David J Sesma, Special Agent FBI

Subscribed and sworn before me this 1st day of December 2016:

KENDALL J NEWMAN, UNITED STATES MAGISTRATES JUDGE

Approved as to form: Matthew D Segal, Heiko P Coppola, Jeremy J Kelly, Assistant United States Attorneys

1 PHILLIP A. TALBERT
   United States Attorney
2 MATTHEW D. SEGAL
   HEIKO P. COPPOLA
3 JEREMY J. KELLEY
   Assistant United States Attorneys
4 501 I Street, Suite 10-100
   Sacramento, CA 95814
5 Telephone: (916) 554-2700
   Facsimile: (916) 554-2900
6

7 Attorneys for Plaintiff
   United States of America
8

FILED

DEC - 8 2016

CLERK, U.S. DISTRICT COURT
EASTERN DISTRICT OF CALIFORNIA
BY _____ DEPUTY CLERK

9   IN THE UNITED STATES DISTRICT COURT

10   EASTERN DISTRICT OF CALIFORNIA

11   2: 1 6 - CR - 0 2 2 7 JAM

12 UNITED STATES OF AMERICA,   CASE NO.

13   Plaintiff,   18 U.S.C. § § 7(1) and 1111 – First Degree Murder
                                       (2 counts)
14   v.

15 SILAS DUANE BOSTON,

16   Defendant.

17

18

19   I N D I C T M E N T

20 COUNT ONE: [18 U.S.C. §§ 7(1) and 1111 – First Degree Murder]

21   The Grand Jury charges: T H A T

22   SILAS DUANE BOSTON,

23 defendant herein, between in or about June 1978 and in or about July 1978, on the high seas and on the

24 Justin B., a vessel belonging in whole and in part to a citizen of the United States, within the special

25 maritime and territorial jurisdiction of the United States, did willfully, deliberately, maliciously and with

26 premeditation and malice aforethought, unlawfully kill Christopher Farmer, a human being, in violation

27 of Title 18, United States Code, Sections 7(1) and 1111.

28

INDICTMENT   1

124

1 | COUNT TWO: [18 U.S.C. §§ 7(1) and 1111 – First Degree Murder]

2 | The Grand Jury further charges: T H A T

3 | SILAS DUANE BOSTON,

4 | defendant herein, between in or about, June 1978 and in or about July 1978, on the high seas and on the

5 | Justin B., a vessel belonging in whole and in part to a citizen of the United States, within the special

6 | maritime and territorial jurisdiction of the United States, did willfully, deliberately, maliciously and with

7 | premeditation and malice aforethought, unlawfully kill Peta Frampton, a human being, in violation of

8 | Title 18, United States Code, Sections 7(1) and 1111.

A TRUE BILL.

/s/ Signature on file w/AUSA

FOREPERSON

PHILLIP A. TALBERT
United States Attorney

125

No. _ _ _ _ _ _ _ _ _

UNITED STATES DISTRICT COURT

Eastern District of California

Criminal Division

THE UNITED STATES OF AMERICA

vs.

SILAS DUANE BOSTON

NO PROCESS NECESSARY

INDICTMENT

VIOLATION(S): 18 U.S.C. § § 7(1) AND 1111 – FIRST DEGREE MURDER
(2 COUNTS)

A true bill,

/s/ Signature on file w/AUSA
_ _
Foreman.

Filed in open court this _ _ _ _ _ _ _ _ _ _ _ _ _ _ *day*

of _ _ _ _ _ _ _ _ _ _ _ _ _ _ *, A.D. 20* _ _ _ _ _

_ _
Clerk.

NO PROCESS NECESSARY _ _   *Carolyn Delaney*
_ _

Carolyn K. Delaney
U.S. Magistrate Judge
GPO 863 525

<u>**United States v. Silas Duane Boston**</u>
Penalties for Indictment

COUNT 1:

VIOLATION: 18 U.S.C. § 1111(a) – First Degree Murder

PENALTIES: Death or Life imprisonment

COUNT 2:

VIOLATION: 18 U.S.C. § 1111(a) – First Degree Murder

PENALTIES: Death or Life imprisonment

SPECIAL ASSESSMENT: $100 (mandatory on each count)

$2) 6 · CR · 0 2 2 7$ JAM

It will be seen that my original strong suspicion that it was Boston who had posted Peta's last letter was finally confirmed by his son Russell Boston. But, having posted it to make it appear Christopher and Peta were alive on 18 June, after Boston would claim to have parted company with them, he had inadvertently really committed a very serious error of judgement. Peta's letter, of course, contained a lot of critical information. In the absence of that last letter, the only brief mention of Boston and *The Justin B* by Peta was in the letter that had preceded it. In the absence of the last letter, nothing could have been known of the visit to Hunting Cay and the meeting with the lighthouse keeper there. Nor would it have been known of a changed travel plan, following the lighthouse keeper's advise to not sail for Puerto Cortes, but instead to head for Livingston. The finding of two unidentified bodies at Punta de Manabique, quite some distance from their original planned destinations, if still somehow actually learned of during enquiries, might never have been thought to be connected with the missing pair. The overall picture of the most important movements of *The Justin B*, as illustrated on my map, would likely never have become known. The plain fact is that without the information in Peta's letter, enquiries to try to trace them would almost certainly have taken place in entirely the wrong places. Boston, in posting that letter, had indeed made a colossal blunder. He provided the necessary clues that were eventually to help reveal the whole horrible truth. Trying to be smart by posting a letter he really ought to have destroyed, was eventually to help prove to be his undoing, albeit very many years later. Before posting that letter he really should have paused to think things through. After all, he did read it!

And so, Boston, the original suspect for those cruel murders in 1978, was finally arrested on December 1, 2016. Aged 75 years at the time, he then appeared before a Grand

Jury at the United States District Court, Eastern District of California in Sacramento, on 8th December 2016. He was taken from his jail cell into the courtroom in a wheelchair and looked every one of his 75 years, presenting with a large bushy white beard and wearing spectacles. His defence attorney Lexi Nagin told the court that Boston was quite deaf and considerable difficulty had been encountered by the attorney when she was trying to communicate with him following his arrest. That was due to Boston not having been supplied with batteries for his hearing aid. During the hearing, Boston did not say anything at all but simply nodded when asked a question to confirm something. On that date, the 8th December 2016, Boston was Indicted by that Grand Jury, comprised of Sacramento citizens, after they were told of the main circumstances of the case and the main reasons the US prosecutors believed that he was the murderer of Christopher and Peta.

The most damning evidence against Boston, of course, came from his two sons, Vincent and Russell Boston and additionally from Bryan Logsdon. I learned that Vince presented as quite an easy subject, on the interview, as was the case with Bryan Logsdon. Russell Boston, however, although providing the evidence he did, seems to have presented as somewhat heavily troubled and less easy to interview than Vincent. Whether, despite everything, Russell was in any way torn between what was required from him and an element of loyalty to his father, can only be guessed at. Below are photographs that appeared in various US and world newspapers, of Vincent Boston, his brother Russell and also Bryan Logsdon. Following that are two photographs of Silas Duane Boston, the first one being as he would have appeared around the time of the murders, and the second which is believed to have been taken not very long prior to his arrest:

VINCE BOSTON

RUSSELL BOSTON

BRYAN LOGSDON

**SILAS DUANE BOSTON
AS HE WOULD HAVE APPEARED AT THE TIME
OF THE MURDERS OF CHRISTOPHER AND PETA**

SILAS DUANE BOSTON
SHORTLY BEFORE HIS ARREST

Detective Sergeant Bob McCloskey, and later Amy
Crosby, did have the original 1968 missing persons' file on
Mary Lou Boston. It is clear that quite exhaustive enquiries
were made by the Sacramento Police to try to discover what
might have happened to her. It indicated that Mary Lou was
allegedly last seen on or about 1st September 1968. I had
originally presumed, wrongly in the event, that Boston had

reported her missing but it was actually Jeffery Venn, Mary Lou's younger brother, aged 15 at the time, who had done that. The original information I had that gave me a reason to believe that Boston, had reported Mary Lou missing, and had at the same time said that she had gone off with another man simply did not seem to sound right. Why would he report her as missing at all if he knew she was with another man? It certainly crossed my mind though, that if Mary Lou's body was later discovered, Boston could then claim she must have been killed by that other man.

In the event, it was only far more recently that I learned that Mary Lou had been reported missing by Jeffery. The original missing report was made on 11th September 1968 and the officer who received the report was Sergeant Bob McCloskey. It seems that shortly before going to the Police and reporting his sister missing, Jeffery had spoken to Boston and became increasingly suspicious, to the degree that he was sure Boston had done his sister harm. Jeffery told the Police that Boston had for a long time possessed a rifle with a mounted scope, said to be his favourite possession but the weapon had disappeared. When asked about the gun, Boston had said he had traded it for some junk items he wanted. Jeffery did not believe that Mary Lou had gone off with another man and neither did Mary Lou's parents who had also told the Police on a number of occasions that they were convinced Mary Lou had been harmed by Boston. Neither they nor Jeffrey believed the other man's story at all, the principle reason being that she was absolutely devoted to her children. Further, all her clothing and personal effects such as her cosmetics were still at her home. Police enquiries though did reveal that Mary Lou had been dating one or two other men, presumably because her marriage to Boston was troubled. Boston was certainly of undoubtedly questionable character in the eyes of the Police but it seems that they concluded there was insufficient evidence to warrant Boston's arrest. One officer felt that he thought Mary Lou had indeed left Boston of her own volition as the marriage was in difficulties.

It will be recalled that Boston told Sergeant Kelly that he had travelled to a place he referred to as "Astar", actually El Estor, this being confirmed by Boston's son Russell, who said they had gone there for about a week. It would appear Boston and his sons sailed there sometime on or just after 6th July 1978 and afterwards sailed back to Livingston, so as to be back there on 16th or 17th July when Boston asserted he made his telephone call to the US. Why Boston made the decision to go to El Estor, an extremely remote and somewhat unattractive place, may not be such a mystery. After committing the murders, I believed that Boston would likely have wanted to put some distance between himself and the murder scene, and thus "lie low" for a time, seemingly a not unusual thing for him to do. To sail to El Estor, from Livingston, though, *The Justin B* first had to enter the wide estuary of the Rio (river) Dulce and then sail generally eastwards to where it narrows to become a river about 100 metres or so wide. The river Dulce then winds for several miles before it opens out into a large, approximately 12 miles long body of water. The boat would have to sail the length of this large lake to where it also narrows to become another roughly 100 metres wide river again. After winding several more miles, the river opens out again to become an enormous inland lake called Lago de Izabal. El Estor lies at the far

136

northeast bank of this lake and the total journey to there from Livingston via the river is certainly of the order of some 45 to 50 miles. I would guess *The Justin B* could have taken perhaps two days to complete the journey, involving an overnight stop somewhere en route. Boston and his sons, after their time spent in El Estor, then had to sail back again, each journey probably involving alternate use of the boat's engine on the narrow stretches, as well as the sails on the open stretches of water. My map of the whole relevant area shows the remote location of El Estor, and also indicates the only route *The Justin B* could possibly have taken to get there from Livingston which lies adjacent to the mouth of the river Dulce estuary. It does seem that there was no other logical way that Boston and his sons could at the time have travelled to El Estor other than on *The Justin B*, there being no proper paved roads nor any public transport. Access from Livingston to El Estor was, and probably still is, almost entirely via the river.

I have to say that subsequent to me having sent my original report and copy file of documents to the US in 1979, for the purpose of the case being followed up, and later learning that neither Vince nor Russell had ever been interviewed, I was astounded. I was also quite angry at that time, and not just for myself, but for the families of Christopher and Peta. I could not help but feel that they had been badly let down. I felt let down too after all my efforts to trace them, learning that they had been murdered, and the fact that there was a very clear suspect. I could never have conceived a similar thing happening, or rather not happening, if the boot had been on the other foot and The Greater Manchester Police had similarly received such a case from the United States. I guess we will never know all the real reasons why the case involving the murders of Christopher and Peta was allowed to stall and "go cold". However, I more recently had to consider that, had Vince and Russell actually been interviewed those years ago, they would probably not have freely confessed that they had actually witnessed the killings. This was because we were to learn very much later that they lived in mortal fear of their father. Despite that, had the boys been interviewed, there might have existed the possibility that the demeanour of one or both of them might have given officers the impression that they were stressed and perhaps hiding something.

In a practical sense, I wondered how the two boys might have easily been interviewed by the Police without Boston having prior knowledge. It is beyond doubt that Boston would have primed them as to what they were to say to the Police if they ever came to be questioned. I thought it possible though, that the boys might then not have actually been living all the time with Boston, but with a relative, perhaps their grandmother. If that had been the case then access to the boys without Boston having prior knowledge, might not have been a problem. During his children's lives, Boston had travelled to Mexico and elsewhere on a number of occasions, most usually to "lie low", when the Police were seeking him for one thing or another. It follows that the children, during such times, would be looked after by Mary Lou but after she disappeared, they would need caring for by someone else. I thought it very likely that the someone else would have been their grandmother which, after Boston's wife disappeared, did prove to be the case.

It will be realised that Bryan Logsdon, a boyhood friend of Russell Boston, was similarly very young at the time of the murders. His future travels with Boston in Mexico, where he was eventually to hear Boston's confessions of several killings, were not to occur until some years into the future.

In February 2017, a court date for Boston's trial still remained to be set and everyone concerned just had to wait until that occurred. I had initially been informed that the US prosecutions team might need me to travel to Sacramento to give evidence, first before a Grand Jury hearing with a view to Boston being indicted (sent for trial) and again later at the trial itself. They also initially desired similar evidence from Audrey Farmer and also no doubt the evidence of the other elderly witnesses who lived in Guatemala and Belize. In the event, that did not happen as Boston was indicted by the Grand Jury on the basis of the Affidavit of FBI Agent David Sesma and the sworn evidence within it.

I was later advised that my evidence for the trial, and that of the other elderly witnesses, would probably first be taken and recorded on video. Mrs Audrey Farmer was by then 92 years old and, at that time in 2017, I was 81 years old. The idea was to secure the sworn evidence of all the elderly witnesses' evidence videotape, obviously in the event that any of us should expire or might be too unwell or infirm to travel to give our "live" evidence at the trial itself, whenever that might eventually be. The process of video recording of our evidence would include the opportunity of cross-examination by Boston's defence attorney at that time.

Audrey Farmer, the mother of Christopher, despite her age of 92 was desperately anxious to go to Sacramento see justice done before she died. Indeed, she was absolutely determined to do so. Audrey, conscious of her age and the passing of time, was moved to write to the court urgently requesting that the trial take place sooner, rather than later. This is an extract of what she wrote:

"…My husband and I were very much involved in the search for them and we did all that we could to establish how, why and who killed them. It is a matter of great sadness that my husband Charles died three years ago never knowing the truth surrounding their deaths and that the murderer was never brought to justice. I am myself now 92 years old…there may be little time left for justice to be seen."

In a court motion, Assistant United States Attorney Mathew D Segal submitted Audrey Farmer's letter to the court, and also a second letter from Christopher's sister Penelope Farmer similarly seeking a trial for Boston to take place as soon as was possible. In her own letter, Penny was said to have written as follows:

"…Making the journey from Oxfordshire, England to travel over 5,200 miles to Sacramento is the very last thing she (Audrey Farmer) can do for Chris."

Mr Segal said to the court, "Christopher Farmer's survivors want to see a trial badly enough that they are willing to travel to Sacramento at risk to the elderly Mrs Farmer's health. Given Audrey farmer's advanced age, justice delayed may be justice permanently denied." Despite this, Audrey Farmer had declared that she "would go to Sacramento for the trial even if they have to carry me onto the 'plane."

To this, Attorney Ms Lexi Negin, Boston's Attorney, and one of Boston's Federal Public Defenders said that Boston, who has arthritis and other health issues is, "Suffering in Sacramento County Jail and is not getting the care he was getting in the nursing home, adding, the defence needs extensive time to prepare his case." Asked by Judge Mendez when the defence would be ready, Negin replied, "Our position is that we will be ready for trial someday." Judge Mendez responded, "That's incredibly unhelpful." When pressed by the Judge for a date when the defence would be ready, Negin suggested the fall of 2018. Judge Mendez, clearly still very unimpressed, retorted, "That's not going to work." The judge then went on to suggest that he was more likely to set a trial date for the fall of 2017, adding, "I think both sides can anticipate this trial will take place this year."

On learning of this court exchange, it might be difficult for some people to initially see why Boston's defence team should really need the better part of two years to prepare his defence. It was evident that Boston intended to plead not guilty despite the huge weight of evidence against him. It had only taken the prosecutors about a year in the rather more onerous task of getting together and assessing all the evidence they needed, and to prepare their case. The defence had all the resulting documents and facts but of course, they did need adequate time to review and assess the prosecution's evidence and to prepare the defence position. It may not be too difficult to think just why Boston's lawyers, should want the start of the trial to be delayed for as long as was possible. Bearing in mind my own age and that of Mrs Farmer and some of the others, could it possibly have been that during a contrived lengthy delay for the start of the trial, one or more of the key elderly witnesses might die? The defence, as well as the prosecution, would recognise that such eventualities might conceivably weaken the prosecution case. Conversely, it could help Boston's defence position. It certainly seems that Judge Mendez thought that two years to prepare the defence was not only ridiculous, he might have also thought it to be a somewhat cynical ploy for the possible reasons suggested above. That is exactly why the prosecuting attorneys wanted the evidence of all the elderly witnesses secured on video prior to the trial, to which the Judge agreed.

Sacramento City's local newspaper, The Sacramento Bee, began reporting details of the case right from the time of Boston's arrest. Peter Hecht, the Bee's reporter was apparently the first to pick up the story and he followed and reported on the case extensively and accurately from that point on. Many other newspapers around the world soon picked up on what was obviously regarded as a sensational story, including The Manchester Evening News and BBC television. A newspaper reporter, probably Peter Hecht, somehow managed to contact and speak to at least one of Boston's two sons following the arrest of their father. The identity of the son was not disclosed but I concluded it doubtless was Vincent. The short newspaper read as follows:

"This is a post in the Sacramento Bee from one of the boys who were on the boat on which the young Brits were allegedly murdered: "…Yes, he threw them both overboard while they were still alive. Then afterwards, he planned to kill me and my brother as well. It was a miracle that we were able to escape alive. He had already killed my mom and has no conscience about killing other people as well. I have been trying to report this to relevant authorities for years, only to be ignored. He almost got away with all these murders as he is 75 years old and probably won't live much longer. This is the tip of the iceberg. There is a lot more that will be revealed."

During my own original enquiries, I had first learned from Charles Farmer, about *The Justin B* having been purchased with a financial contribution from Boston's father, Russell Boston. Whether that was to assist Boston in evading the authorities in connection with the ongoing rape allegation, or something else, was not known. One supposes that he could have simply gone off to Mexico again rather than buy a boat. What was later learned was that the Boston family, and perhaps other people too, knew that Boston had murdered Mary Lou, this having been regarded as a "family secret." It is quite reasonable to assume, I believe, that if Boston's sons knew this awful secret, as did their grandmother, then Boston's father probably also knew his son was a murderer. I learned, during an early meeting with Charles Farmer, that whilst he had been making his own enquiries, prior to my involvement, he had spoken on the telephone to Russell Boston senior. He had thought at first, by asking the question, "Mr Boston?" and getting an affirmative answer, that he was talking to Silas Boston himself. Mr Farmer had taperecorded that conversation and handed me a copy of it. When, after a minute or two, it became apparent that he was actually talking to Boston's father, he had asked him if he knew Boston's whereabouts as he needed to speak to him about Christopher and Peta who had been with him on *The Justin B*. Boston senior appeared friendly and cooperative on the recording and said he would try to make contact with his son for Mr Farmer. That conversation did result in Boston telephoning Mr Farmer from California, full details of which have already been referred to. I have since been left to wonder, though, whether Boston Senior might himself have suspected or known his son as having been involved in the reason for the disappearance of Christopher and Peta, considering he probably knew his son had murdered Mary Lou and maybe others. Boston, having freely boasted to Bryan Logsdon, about killing Mary Lou, Christopher, Peta and others, he might well have also confided those things to his father as well as to his mother who also certainly knew he had killed her daughter in law.

Bearing in mind that Boston did ring Mr Farmer as a result of the earlier conversation between Boston's father and Mr Farmer, could it possibly have been the case that after a "discussion" between Boston and his father, Boston senior advised his son that it might be a good idea to ring Mr Farmer back with a view to appearing helpful, so as to try to alleviate any suspicions?

I had presumed that Boston's sons had disclosed to Detective Crosby what they knew on the lead up to Boston's arrest but I had to wait to find out what that was. I was eventually to learn everything from the contents of the Affidavit of FBI Agent David Sesma which pretty well filled in many of the gaps in this horror story. The assertion that previous attempts had been made by one of Boston's sons to report his father's crimes to the relevant authorities, but that such attempts had seemingly been ignored, was extremely worrying. It was probably the case though, that it had been concluded there appeared no evidence to support the allegations. Just because a person alleges that he suspects or knows someone has committed a crime, is usually quite insufficient proof in itself because, unless the offence is admitted by the person accused, it amounts to one person's word against another's. Therefore, the Police would usually need more evidence to support or corroborate the accuser's evidence. However, such corroborative evidence is frequently not readily apparent unless it is actively sought. It is completely accepted that repeated attempts were made by

Vince to draw Police attention to the activities of Boston but it is also apparent that there was just no supporting evidence at the time, nor for a long time afterwards. Vince Boston, however, could quite understandably have been left with the impression that not enough had ever been done, or that he had been ignored.

In early February 2017, I learned that Boston's lawyers had been informed by Sacramento Jail officials, that Boston had been taken ill and admitted to hospital. For security reasons, the Jail refused to state which hospital Boston had been taken to. His lawyers suggested that Boston was suffering from "a very serious condition", adding, "we are unsure if he is talking or conscious." Boston was due another court appearance on Monday 13th February 2017 when it was hoped Judge Mendez would set a court date but when Boston did not appear, that did not happen. Lexi Negin, Boston's defence Attorney, said that Boston was suffering from, "Complications of liver failure and congestive heart failure". On the face of things, this sounded very serious of course but being something of a cynical old Detective, I did wonder whether Boston's stated condition was really quite as serious as was being suggested. I wondered whether what everyone was being led to understand, might simply be little more than a contrived delaying tactic.

Prior to the arrangement being finally made for evidence of the elderly witnesses to be secured via video link between the US and England, Federal prosecutors, hoping to speed up Boston's trial, had originally wanted Judge Mendez to approve in-court depositions for the relatives of Christopher Farmer, including his 92-year-old mother, Audrey, sister Penny, myself and the others from Guatemala and Belize. In a written motion to the court, Attorney Matthew Segal at that time had asked that the pre-trial depositions should be taken in open court, arguing: "There is no better evidence than sworn, crossexamined testimony taken under court supervision. Given the witnesses' current ability and willingness to travel, there is no practical reason why their depositions cannot be taken under the conditions that the law most favours."

However, Boston's defence Attorney argued, for some reason that was not readily apparent, that "any pre-trial depositions should be conducted in private and not introduced into the record until the trial begins." In response, Judge Mendez scheduled a hearing for February 28, 2017, to get an update on Boston's medical condition and to consider an anticipated motion by prosecutors to allow the depositions even if Boston could not be present in court himself.

This arrangement having been decided, Detective Clinch advised me that Boston had been discharged from hospital a day or so after 13th February and returned to Sacramento Jail. She emailed me this information after I had earlier emailed a message to her in which I had also mentioned that I hoped a Police guard was in place at the hospital where Boston was being held. This was because I suspected that Boston, despite his 75 years, was prospectively just as crafty as ever and, if actually well enough, he just might hope for an opportunity to arise to enable him to escape from the hospital. From what I had been led to understand, Boston was someone who was quite practised at evading the US Law Enforcement authorities in the past, by "lying low" in Mexico and other places in Central America, including of course Belize and Guatemala where he fled to evade an alleged US Federal Rape offence. I was much reassured to learn soon afterwards that Boston was back in Sacramento Jail.

It was thought wise by someone, pending the trial, that there should be no direct contact between myself and Audrey or Penny. I did not agree with that decision as I thought, with my background and considerable experience, in applying to me, it was unnecessarily over-cautious. Indeed, I was slightly resentful at that suggestion. I saw no reason how, with my background and experience, anyone would possibly think I would ever disclose anything confidential, or that anything I might be prepared to discuss with Audrey or Penny could possibly jeopardise the case in the slightest. Most of the important case details had anyway already been published and very widely reported worldwide in the press and online. In addition, the full affidavit of the FBI Agent David Sesma was published on the web for anyone and everyone to see. In the event, there was no contact between us although I did know from Detective Clinch that Audrey Farmer and Penny certainly did want to meet with me to express their gratitude.

On 12th January 2017 Penny sent a very cordial and warm thank you e-mail message to me via Michaela Clinch concerning my original and continuing involvement in this case. The first copies of this book reproduced the whole text of her very nice simple message but Penny, for her own reasons, later asked that it be removed. In accordance with her wish, I did so and therefore her message did not appear in the later amended editions of the printed, or e-book.

Peter Hecht, the Sacramento Bee reporter filed the following story, published online by the paper, on Tuesday 28th February 2017:

"Silas Duane Boston, out of the hospital after apparent complications from heart and liver disease, returned to federal court Tuesday (28th) as a judge approved pre-trial depositions and set a tentative October date for Boston to face trial for the 1978 murders of two British tourists who were allegedly hogtied and thrown from his boat into the Caribbean Sea. He is also is being investigated in the 1968 disappearance of his former wife, Mary Lou Boston, who authorities believe was murdered and buried near a remote Northern California creek. Her body has never been found. As the investigation continues, Boston, who turned 76 on March 20th 2017, appeared in court in a wheelchair as United States District Judge John A Mendez agreed to schedule depositions in April or May for four aging witnesses in the Caribbean murder case. Authorities say they want their testimony on the record as soon as possible in case they don't live long enough to take the witness stand in Boston's trial. One of those witnesses was Audrey Farmer, 92 years, who lived in the county of Oxfordshire, England, whose son, medical school graduate Christopher Farmer, was killed along with girlfriend Peta Frampton. The United States Authorities also intended to call Farmer's sister, Penelope Farmer, as well as a British law enforcement official and a forensic scientist from Guatemala who carried out the post mortem examinations on the recovered bodies. In a February 14th motion, United States prosecuting Attorney Phillip A Talbert asked Mendez to hold the depositions "in a trial-like setting, i.e. held in an open court, on the record and open to the public, thereby affording the public their proper access to the proceedings." Mendez approved the motion to schedule the depositions but rejected the prosecution's request to hold them in open court. "I do not intend to have a judge or a magistrate sit (in a courtroom) and have them appear as witnesses for a trial," he said. The judge said the prosecution may interview the witnesses and record their testimony for potential introduction for trial with the defence allowed to crossexamine them. He said the depositions were to be conducted at a location to be determined by the lawyers. A federal magistrate would be available to answer procedural questions by phone but wouldn't be physically present. Mendez set a potential trial date for October 2nd but said he was uncertain the case would be ready to begin with jury selection by then. "I'm not setting a trial date yet," he said. "It's only tentative." Boston, equipped with headphones to help his hearing, said he was having trouble following the discussion. "Were you able to hear me, Mr Boston?" Mendez asked. Boston nodded to the judge but indicated he couldn't hear his attorney, federal public defender Lexi Negin. "I couldn't hear her," he said, fumbling with his headgear. "Hello? Hello?" Negin, who on February 14th said Boston was hospitalised for nearly two weeks for a very serious condition, indicated her client had actually improved. Mendez approved a defence motion to be allowed confidential access to interview Boston at Sacramento County Jail. "He is taking a lot of medication," Nagin said. "Mr Boston is good today. I don't think there is any issue today. But it is an on-going medical issue." At that point, Boston was due back in court on June 6th 2016.

On 24th March 2017, I received an email from the Greater Manchester Cold Case Department to ask if I would be able to fly to California on Saturday 6th May 2017. Audrey Farmer and her daughter Penny were apparently to go on the same flight. Penny could also look after her mother, who although somewhat frail, was extremely keen to go. Although there were direct flights to San Francisco from Manchester, we were all apparently going to fly from Heathrow in London as Audrey and Penny lived in the south of England. Michaela Clinch and Martin Bottomley were also going and so we, from the north, would need to travel down to London on 5th June so as to be there for the flight on the 6th. We had all obtained our Visa Waiver ESTAs, to actually allow us to enter the United States and, as the travel date drew very near, I got out my suitcase with a view to starting to put a few things into it. It appeared that we were all to be met at San Francisco Airport and then driven the eighty or so miles to Sacramento where hotel reservations had been made. I must confess that it was all quite exciting and I was looking forward to it enormously.

In Sacramento, it was decided that Audrey and I would be required to give our videoed testimony which would then be subject to crossexamination by Boston's Attorney. Whether Boston himself would be able to attend the proceedings was unknown of course but I dearly wanted to be able to look at him, and for him to look at me. The necessary arrangements being in hand, it was reassuring to know our evidence, once secured on video, should any one of us be unable to go, our evidence would be admissible at the eventual trial for the jury to hear and see. So, we were all on standby to travel the thousands of miles to Sacramento on 6th May 2017 to give our testimony and were due to return home on 13th. Leastwise, that was the plan. However, on the 24th April 2017, when my wife Jane and I were visiting relatives in Scotland, Detective Clinch sent me the following message which I actually picked up a little later:

"I left a message on your answerphone on Friday, just to make you aware that Boston had taken a turn for the worse and next of kin were being called to the hospital. We have had no further updates but I will let you know as and when anything changes…"

I was also advised in the message that as a result of this development, our intended travel arrangements for 6th May were consequently on hold. I must say that I was beginning to get a very bad feeling. That bad feeling was fully borne out when, on 25th April 2017, I picked up the following deeply unwelcome further message on our return home from Scotland:

"Good morning David. Well, it's happened… We received an email from the US in the early hours of this morning to say that Silas Duane Boston died in hospital at 17.09 hours Pacific Daylight Time on Monday 24th April 2017. As you will be fully aware this, sadly, brings the re-investigation to a close, just as we were getting there…

I know we were expecting this, but I also know you will be so disappointed after all your hard work on the original investigation, and I would just like to say thank you once again on behalf of the Cold Case Review Unit for all of your invaluable help and co-operation—not all retired officers are so keen to get involved. The Farmer family are devastated right now as you can imagine, so it's not appropriate to set up any sort of meeting just yet but I'll be in touch when they are ready if that's all right.

Hello to Jane and have a safe journey home today,
Michaela"

So, after everything, Boston never actually stood trial and some might be of the view that his death enabled him to escape justice. However, it must be said that shortly after I received the original surprise telephone call from Detective Clinch on 5th October 2015, I had asked her if Boston was actually still alive. I knew he would be 75 years old at that time. The reply shortly afterwards was that he was indeed still alive and so enquiries could commence by US Law Enforcement. Had Boston not been alive, then the whole thing would have ended there and then. There could have been no re-investigation and that meant the full truth concerning the deaths of Christopher Farmer and Peta Frampton, as has been described, would never have emerged. And anyway, what could possibly have happened had I never kept all those copy documents?

But Boston was still alive and the full dreadful truth was revealed by the investigation. But did Boston, in dying before his intended trial, truly escape justice? Many people might think so but I do not actually share such a view. Boston was undoubtedly not well at the time of his arrest and my firm belief was that his arrest, after so many years, came as a colossal shock to his system, both physically and mentally. He was, after being indicted, then held in custody for some five months during which period he must have suffered enormous building stress as he came to realise the final hopelessness of his situation. He must have realised that, in the face of the damning evidence of his guilt, his impending trial was almost a formality. A guilty plea by him or a finding of guilt meant he would spend the remaining days of his life locked up. That original shock, subsequent stress, and the realisation of the hopelessness of his situation quite probably destroyed all his physical and mental resistance and he effectively started to simply shut down and then died. I did hear from one source that Boston had stopped taking his medication before he died. And Silas Duane Boston did not die a free man. He died in custody although it is true he had enjoyed so many years of freedom after committing those cruel murders at Punta de Manabique. Even if he had remained alive and had been convicted, his time in prison serving his sentence would likely not have been very long. So, either before or after a trial, Boston did not have long to live. I was quite content despite his death before his trial and I hoped that the families of the victims would at least draw some final comfort in the knowledge that the utter brute who carried out those cruel murders was finally arrested and died in custody.

There are of course more victims in this case than poor Christopher Farmer and Peta Frampton. Audrey Farmer, aged 92 at the time of writing, is still suffering from the loss of her son in such awful circumstances, as are Christopher's Siblings, Penny and Nigel. The Frampton families also suffered dreadfully. Additional victims are of course Vince and Russell Boston who had, incredibly, learned from Boston himself that he had brutally shot their mother dead when they were small children. Added to that was the horror of the cold-blooded murders that they were, as children, forced to witness whilst aboard *The Justin B* on that awful day in 1978 but had never dared to speak about. Further, throughout their lives since, they had to live with an inevitable inbuilt sense of guilt in having to suppress that knowledge whilst continuing to live in utter terror of their father. They well knew what Silas Duane Boston was capable of doing to people he was offended by. It is to be hoped that the two brothers, Vince and Russell can now live the rest of their lives in a much-improved state of mind, having finally been able to unburden themselves and no longer live in fear.

After the death of his father, Vince Boston was moved to place the post below on the internet. I should explain that the terms EAR and ONS he mentioned in his post at that time, referred to a man known as the East Area Rapist (EAR) and the Original Night Stalker (ONS), also known as the Diamond Knot Killer & the Golden State Killer. When Vince placed his post, & during the time I was writing this book, that prolific dangerous criminal was still at large. However, in 2018 Joseph DeAngelo, 74 years, an ex-police officer, was arrested in Sacramento whilst living in retirement. He later pleaded guilty, apparently to avoid the death penalty, & was sentenced to life imprisonment with no possibility of parole, for a number of dreadful crimes, including multiple murders.

Vince wrote as follows:

Jun 18, 2017 at 5.02am

"I've been following this blog for a bit, and because my father has died, I am no longer in danger of muddying the jury pool by making a public statement. Yes, my father Silas Duane Boston was suspected of being the EAR, ONS... For a while, he was the number one suspect due to his similarities... Height, age, MO of burglaries and home invasions, ski mask and burglary tools and techniques in Sacramento at the same time, murder, marksman and weapons expert, ex Coast Guard, ex-Vietnam vet, former ambulance attendant and surgeon's assistant, American River College student in the early 1970s, worked as a maintenance worker for a real estate company in Sacramento and Carmichael and places we've lived as well as dates, (we moved to 57th street and Folsom Blvd in June of 1976), show size, piercing blue eyes, a tattoo of a mermaid on his left forearm, propensity for killing others who crossed him as well as the murder of the British couple in front of me and my brother when we were kids, then nearly killing us a couple of weeks later to ensure we wouldn't snitch on him. Also, several other Southern California connections in Irvine, Dana Point and Los Angeles etc. The evidence was so compelling…for a couple of months in 2016, I wondered if it was him. But the DNA evidence has ruled him out. Also, we were in Belize when some of the rapes occurred, but they did taper off and move out of Sacramento in late 1977, exactly when we left for Belize.

My father was a bad person and a prolific criminal, there's no denying that. He was actually much worse as I have learned from the recent investigation. But he's not the EAR, (at least not the specific DNA POI).

The Sacramento Police Department did an incredible job in the investigation of my father. He's been an expert at evading the authorities all these years, and if not for the EAR investigation, the Sacramento Missing Persons' detectives and the FBI realising he was an uncaught serial killer, then connected the dots on how they could get jurisdiction for a 1978 double murder in Guatemala, my father would never have been arrested. Contrary to the newspaper articles, my brother and I as well as countless other people have been reporting my father to the authorities, police, FBI, Interpol etc for over 30 years, but through numerous lost files and jurisdictional issues, he has eluded justice. It's not like the movies and it's truly amazing how many times he fell between the cracks and got away through the years, just by moving and hiding out until investigations grew cold.

Yes, he did kill my mother Mary Lou Boston and he told us so. It was a "family secret" everyone knew about but kept under wraps. He also killed several other people in the course of his crimes, drug deals gone bad, people he said deserved it and numerous other people. I can't help but think about all the people who would still be alive if he had been incarcerated for my mom's 1968 murder, but as I said, it's not the movies, investigations aren't buttoned up in an hour-long episode and prolific criminals learn from time and experience. I hope the EAR is caught or identified because his victims deserve the closure which can only come from their tormentor being incarcerated, or identified as deceased.

I didn't even know the weight of the fear I had for my father until after he died and it wasn't there anymore. Only then did I realise he would never again come and threaten me or extort money from me by threatening to harm others if I didn't comply. Because so many people knew about my father and his crimes through the years, I believe there are people who know who the EAR is, perhaps not directly, but as a friend, neighbour, relative, co-worker or classmate. Someone who has the missing piece of the puzzle but who have never had the image placed in front of them in a way that creates an, "Oh I know that guy" moment.

The Sacramento PD and the FBI are still working on the case, and I'm hoping through public awareness, the EAR, ONS, Golden State Killer will be caught. In the meantime, thank you for taking the time and effort to solve this case."

Audrey and Penny Farmer were absolutely determined to attend the trial but Boston's death, although initially devastating for them did actually mean that they were spared the ordeal of having to sit in the courtroom and hear some agonising testimony. On hearing of their regret at not having been able to see Boston actually convicted in court, I decided that if possible, I would try to visit them in Oxfordshire in the hope of alleviating their distress, at least to some degree. They had anyway earlier said that they wanted to meet with me to express their gratitude for my own part in the case.

On Friday 7th July 2017, I, therefore, drove down to Oxfordshire to meet with Audrey and Penny, with my wife Jane. We were greeted with smiles and were made to feel welcome. We then spent a couple of hours talking about the case in their lovely garden on what was a warm sunny afternoon. We enjoyed cups of tea and some cake with them as we talked. Their disappointment at the case ending as it did was very clear. Penny in particular still appeared quite unhappy, indeed incredulous that the case had seemingly not originally been properly dealt with by American Law Enforcement. My response was that we would probably never actually know exactly what might have gone wrong but pointed out that evidence discovered during the fresh investigation was simply not available back then. Vince and Russell had lived in terror of their father and because of this, even if they had been interviewed back then, they probably would not have dared to disclose what they had witnessed. Also, Logsdon would not have figured in the matter back then for a very obvious reason. I told Audrey and Penny that my own feelings were that, despite also being disappointed at not seeing Boston convicted, I was totally convinced that a trial could only have resulted in him being found guilty, such was the weight of evidence against him. The result of a guilty finding would have been that Boston, a cold-blooded murderer, would have spent the rest of his days in prison. In the event, he did die in custody following his arrest and it cannot be doubted that the final investigation in the US was an enormous success.

Prior to our arrival, my wife and I had discussed informing Audrey and Penny about my intention to write a book about the case as we perceived it might be a somewhat sensitive issue for them. When I broached it in the garden though, Penny just responded that she had thought to write something herself. As we were about to leave, Penny took a nice photograph of Audrey and me together in the garden, that being at Audrey's request. I later received a message via Penny's email, requesting that I do not use the photograph in my book. In the event, I had not intended doing so. Audrey, I realised afterwards, did not say very much during our meeting, but she was an absolutely charming lady. That came as no surprise to me at all, having been so well acquainted with her husband Charles who was an equally charming gentleman. I am so sorry he did not live to see Boston arrested.

Following an invitation in August 2017, I also went with my wife Jane to visit the GMP Cold Case Unit in Manchester. Michaela Clinch and Martin Bottomley greeted us warmly there and, as might be expected, we spent a little while chatting about the case and drinking tea. Whilst there, Michaela handed me a box that I found contained an official Greater Manchester Police Plaque. She then made a request concerning what they would like to happen to the plaque. A photograph of it is reproduced here along with a photograph of myself, Michaela and Martin at the Unit.

THE G.M.P. PLAQUE

MARTIN BOTTOMLY DAVID SACKS & MICHAELA CLINCH

What was quite remarkable, so many years after the crime, was that sufficient numbers of the key witnesses and documentary evidence still survived. During a conversation about the murders with a friend, he suggested the case had been somewhat similar to building a jigsaw puzzle as pieces needed to be found and used to build the overall picture in this case. When Michaela Clinch was first contacted by Penny, she became aware of the existence of an old puzzle but initially, she possessed none of the pieces. The first was my name, provided by Audrey's long memory. That should have provided access to other important pieces, all contained in the headquarters file, but it was lost. However, Michaela learned, to her great surprise, that there existed a copy of some critical pieces of the puzzle, those being in my garden shed. That enabled the puzzle to be partly constructed. The other pieces were seemingly thousands of miles away in the US, that is if they could be found. Over there, one by one, they were found. Boston's sons and Bryan Logsdon provided some of the most critical ones. In addition, the FBI found three other pieces, in

Belize and Guatemala, those being one of the Bomberos who recovered the bodies, the retired Doctor who carried out the post mortem examinations, and a port official. The final pieces of the puzzle could finally then be inserted to complete the picture, to reveal the originally suspected murderer as Silas Duane Boston. So, my friend was right, this murder case was indeed similar, like so many others, to a jigsaw puzzle.

Chapter Eight
A Degree of Closure

After everything that had happened, and all the excellent work involved during the investigation, all followed by Boston's death, I somehow still felt there was something missing, something I needed to do for myself. Therefore, on 5th October 2017, my wife Jane and I flew from Manchester to San Francisco. Whilst there, we one day caught a Greyhound bus to Sacramento and spent three days there. Detective Crosby knew of my intention and she had then told all those who had been involved in the US investigation. On Sunday 8th October, whilst in Sacramento, my wife and I received an email from Matthew Segal, one of the US Attorneys who had played such a large part in the case. As a result, at 5 pm that night Matthew came to our hotel, greeted us with obvious pleasure and then first drove us to a bar where predictably we had a beer and a chat. Matthew and I hit it off immediately.

From the bar, we then walked a few yards to a very nice restaurant, for some reason called a cafeteria, where we found six other people already seated at a table waiting for us, all of them with wide smiles on their faces. Jane and I went over with Matthew, sat down and introductions were made. I felt extremely honoured, and so did Jane, that all those people with extremely busy private and work lives had turned out to meet and spend that Sunday evening with us. They were all lovely people and their friendly, relaxed, open and easygoing manner and conversation belied the undoubted enormous joint talent and expertise that was present around that table. I would just love to have been able to work with such people.

Obviously, a few photographs were taken. The first shows me between Amy and Matthew. The second is of Amy Crosby and me, with Amy holding the Greater Manchester Police Plaque I had been handed by Michaela and Martin, who, knowing I was going, had asked me to deliver and present it. The third picture is of all of us there, less Jeremy Kelly's wife Victoria who took the photograph. Victoria told us she was born at Stepping Hill Hospital, Stockport, Manchester where, by way of a small coincidence, my daughter, also called Jane, has worked as a senior radiographer for many years. Nearest the camera on the left is Mathew Segal, then myself with Amy Crosby on my left. Next to Amy at the bottom left of the table is Heiko Coppola. Opposite Heiko is Amy's work partner Janine LeRose with her husband Jerry on her left. Nearest the camera on the right is Jeremy Kelly, with the space to his right where Victoria should be. Between Victoria and Jerry, and opposite me is my wife Jane. Unfortunately, neither of the FBI officers who were involved in the case nor Attorney Philip Talbert could be there. The only thing that saddened Jane and I is the fact that we are unlikely to ever see any of these great people again.

MATTHEW SEGAL, MYSELF & AMY CROSBY

DAVID SACKS AND AMY CROSBY

**THE TEAM MEETING IN SACRAMENTO
8TH OCTOBER 2017**

Not to be outdone by my presentation of the Greater Manchester Police Plaque, Amy immediately responded by presenting me with a Sacramento Police Department badge, a Sacramento Police uniform shoulder badge, and a mug decorated with the Sacramento Police insignia, photographs of which now also follow:

THE SACRAMENTO POLICE BADGE

SACRAMENTO POLICE UNIFORM BADGE

THE POLICE MUG

On 1st November, 2017, I received an email from Amy Crosby. She told me that in February 2018 she and FBI Agent David Sesma were to give a presentation about the case. That presentation was to be at a Las Vegas convention of the California Homicide Investigator's Association during which they intended to use a number of photographs. To add a further piece of light interest, she asked me if I would send her a photograph of my garden shed. I, therefore, sent her the photograph that now follows. I attached to it a few words that may serve to illustrate my everlasting deep embarrassment at the singularly insecure place where documents, that were eventually to prove so critical to a new investigation, had unknowingly lain for so many years. I could kick myself forever confessing to Michaela Clinch the place where I had finally located that old copy file! It crossed my mind that perhaps I should kick Michaela too as she went and blabbed that little gem of information to the US! My shed photograph then finally figured in the Las Vegas case presentation and no doubt resulted in a few smiles and also shaking of some heads.

SECURE STOREAGE FACILITY FOR IMPORTANT AND SENSITIVE DOCUMENTS

Later, FBI Special Agent David Sesma also emailed me to request that I send him photographs of myself whilst serving as a police officer, including one of me in uniform. The request was with a view to using them at the Las Vegas presentation he would be doing with Amy Crosby. He told me it was expected there would likely be around one thousand US Homicide investigators attending the event. I, therefore, sent David Sesma two photographs, one of me as a rather new young constable in uniform age 22, the second being of me as a rather more mature looking detective sergeant in 1968, that being the very year Mary Lou was murdered by Boston:

POLICE CONSTABLE DAVID SACKS
IN 1958

**DETECTIVE SERGEANT DAVID SACKS
IN 1968**

Boston having departed this world, and now having finally been able to write this book without having to invent an ending to an alternative semi-fictional one, I will now return to my retirement trusting I will not receive any more telephone calls from the GMP Cold Case Unit in the future. In the event, I do not have any more old documents anyway, either in the garden shed or anywhere else.

Detective Amy Crosby, and the others involved in the investigation, for some reason, had apparently been looking forward to meeting me when I was originally to fly over for the purpose of giving my testimony at court. They were no doubt curious to see the old oddball ex-cop who had kept a thick pile of mouldering documents in his garden shed for so many years. With the death of Boston, that meeting, as things stood, was obviously not going to take place. So, I decided to make it happen anyway. I thought such a meeting might possibly be a pleasant way to bring some element of closure to the sad unfinished business that this case had represented for me for so many years. And so, it has proved to be! I would still, though, have so much savoured the opportunity to have been able to look Boston in the eyes across the courtroom to try to convey an unspoken message to him, "Got you, you wicked blackhearted bastard!"